THE BAR

THE BAR

A SPIRITED GUIDE TO COCKTAIL ALCHEMY

OLIVIER SAID AND JAMES MELLGREN

TEN SPEED PRESS
Berkeley | Toronto

Ten Speed Press

Box 7123

Berkeley, California 94707

www.tenspeed.com

Distributed in Australia by Simon and Schuster Australia, in Canada by Ten Speed Press Canada, in New Zealand by Southern Publishers Group, in South Africa by Real Books, and in the United Kingdom and Europe by Airlift Book Company.

Cover and text design by James Wilson

Library of Congress Cataloging-in-Publication Data

Said, Olivier,

    The bar / Olivier Said and James Mellgren.

       p. cm.

    ISBN-10: 1-58008-682-9

    ISBN:13: 978-1-58008-682-0

     1.Bartending. 2. Cocktails. I. Mellgren, James. II. Title.

TX951.S25 2005

641.8′74—dc22

              2005049044

Printed in Hong Kong

First printing, 2005

1 2 3 4 5 6 7 8 9 10 — 09 08 07 06 05

To our wives, Megan and Sydney,
for whom we would gladly make cocktails anytime.

OCCUPAI

CONTENTS

ICY 84

ACKNOWLEDGMENTS

James and Olivier would like to thank everyone they have ever known. However, for the sake of brevity we'll stick to a select few who have inspired us, helped us, taught us, or in some way contributed to this book (and whose names we remember).

We want to thank everyone at César with whom we work, but especially owners Dennis Lapuyade and Richard Mazzera, and the extraordinary bartenders, Bill Whiteley, Tim Kampa, Dylan O'Brien, Scott Baird, and our bonny Cate Whalen.

Thanks also to Jose Martin and Alex Conde-Skeels for making all the bartenders look good.

Thanks to César executive chef Maggie Pond because we love her, we respect her, and because we stole her syrup recipe.

We stand in awe of, and wish to thank, our copyeditor, Jasmine Star.

Thanks to all the talented people at Ten Speed who have helped shepherd this book to a shelf near you, our editor Carrie Rodrigues, editorial director Aaron Wehner, and publisher extraordinaire, Phil Wood.

We'd like to thank two wild and crazy distillers who inhabit a strange island called Alameda, Lance Winters and Jörg Rupf, owners of St. George Spirits (makers of Hangar One Vodka).

Olivier would like to thank (and beg for forgiveness from) his wife, Megan, and his son, Archibald.

James would like to make a big Margarita for his wife, Sydney.

And finally, our biggest thanks to the third (and silent) member of our team, James Wilson, our graphic designer for both *The Bar* and *César*. He's not really silent; but with us around, he just can't get a word in edgewise. Jim would like to thank Annette Flores.

d safety of the group. This act of bonding after the sun goes down, so essential to the human conditi
hat the French refer to as soupape de securite, a kind of pressure valve for the soul of the commu
er since humans discovered fermented and distilled spirits, alcohol in one form or another has be
ntegral part of this ritual. This is still true today, only now the ritual is played out in neighbo
rs, fancy cocktail lounges, living rooms, backyard patios, and any number of parties and fest
cross America. At the heart of all this revelry stands the bartender—a combination of short-order
hilosopher, therapist, storyteller, and all-around dispenser of good cheer. Some experienced barte
e fonts of knowledge and lore, while those who are new to the profession are often scrambli

Good

so, in pu
ere asse
gredien
me, a pl
age for re
les acco

hile this
ix drinks
e inform

Cheer

e Egypti
bread th
d as far
turally
still tha

ose who
roughou
ere also p
ith cooki
ere estab
ges that
onaste

nowledge
nerally a
t rather
d arom
here the
forbidde
th come
st of Eu
via, and
ong with
pt the a
nce, the
rmentation

order to make spirits, you first need a fermented liquid, such as wine or beer. Virtually any food
m containing sugars (or starches that can be converted into sugar), can be fermented, and most w
naturally if conditions are right. Although similar to the process of making sourdough bread,
rmentation is a controlled and highly precise science. To this liquid, yeast is added—either naturally
e human hand—and then the action begins. The yeast cells feed off the sugars, devouring them
nverting them into ethanol (ethyl alcohol) and carbon dioxide. This conversion is a violent pro
akes the liquid appear to be boiling. In fact, the word fermentation comes from the Latin word fo
eaning "to boil," an apt description of the party taking place within the vat. When the proc
mpleted, you're left with a fermented brew—wine if grapes or other fruit is used, or beer wh

INTRODUCTION

Hermit hoar, in solemn cell,
Wearing out life's evening gray;
Smite thy bosom, sage, and tell,
What is bliss, and which the way?
Thus I spoke; and speaking sigh'd;
Scarce repressed a starting tear;
When the smiling sage replie'd –
"Come, my lad, and drink some beer."
—Samuel Johnson

WELCOME TO THE BAR

It's no great mystery why for millennia men and women have gathered together at dusk around the communal fire to recount their day, share stories, commiserate, break bread, and seek the warmth and safety of the group. This act of bonding after the sun goes down, so essential to the human condition, is what the French refer to as *soupape de securité*, a kind of pressure valve for the soul of the community. Ever since humans discovered fermented and distilled spirits, alcohol in one form or another has been an integral part of this ritual. This is still true today, only now the ritual is played out in neighborhood bars, fancy cocktail lounges, living rooms, backyard patios, and any number of parties and festivals across America.

At the heart of all this revelry stands the bartender—a combination of short-order cook, philosopher, therapist, storyteller, and all-around dispenser of good cheer. Some experienced bartenders are fonts of knowledge and lore, while those who are new to the profession are often scrambling to learn the difference between single-malt and sloe gin. Still others are weekend bartenders, mixing the occasional Martini or Margarita for friends and family, but wanting to better understand the alchemy and traditions behind their favorite spirits and cocktails.

Eau-de-vie, aquavit, uisge beatha, aqua vitae, zhizennia voda—they may all be made differently (though not all that much), and from different raw materials, but they all mean the same thing, "water of life." Along with wine and beer, distilled spirits in all of their variations are what make up the modern bar. Within this realm of the spirits is a vast amount of information that can be daunting, if not downright overwhelming, to a novice bartender or a fledgling amateur. With that in mind, we hope that The Bar presents a thorough but concise knowledge base—for professionals and amateurs alike—on the ancient tradition of enjoying and mixing spirits.

A GOOD BAR IS HARD TO FIND

Why does one step into a drinking establishment for a cocktail or a shot of whiskey when in most cases it would be just as easy to drink at home? There is no question that the social aspect to drinking is one of its most compelling features, with the idea that after a drink or two you can end up having a spirited conversation with the heretofore complete stranger sitting next to you. The very design of the bar couldn't be more democratic and egalitarian—the plumber sits next to the judge, who sits next to the waiter, who sits next to the teacher, and so on. The bartender stands by as an almost silent witness to the goings-on, ready with the tools and ingredients to produce a bevy of delicious cocktails and an array of spirits, liqueurs, and variously fortified concoctions from all over the world.

Also, in purely economic terms, one can sample a broad range of spirits that would cost a small fortune if they were assembled at home. And for cocktail drinkers, it relieves them of having to keep fresh an assortment of ingredients and garnishes necessary to make proper drinks. For many people, the bar is an extension of the home, a place not only to meet and greet, but to entertain one's friends and family, woo a client, or set the stage for romance. Environment and ambiance are key elements to any bar, and people choose their watering holes accordingly.

We don't know if this is a good thing or a bad thing, but a list of celebrities who are former bartenders includes stars such as Bruce Willis, Sandra Bullock, Bill Cosby, Chevy Chase, Kris Kristofferson, and Tom Arnold. If you count the movie *Cocktail*, you can add Tom Cruise to the list.

NO SMOKING

World explorers have always set their priorities. It is well established that Columbus took casks of sherry with him as he set sail for what he thought would be the East Indies in 1492. Twenty-five years later, as Magellan was preparing to sail around the world, the explorer spent more on sherry than on all the weapons he took with him. Even the Puritans took more beer than water with them aboard the Mayflower. **Puritans indeed.**

While this book is not a definitive study, we believe that the majority of what you need to know in order to mix drinks competently and enjoy the world of spirits can be found within these pages. So here's wishing that the information herein will help provide you with a lifetime of healthy drinking, friendship, and camaraderie. Cheers!

A DISTILLED HISTORY OF ALCOHOL

Alcoholic beverages have been present through virtually every stage of recorded human history, and no doubt long before anyone began to keep score. Who discovered them? We will probably never know for sure, and given that the process of fermentation is a naturally occurring phenomenon, it is very likely that it was discovered by more than one culture. Although somewhat shrouded in time, there are many archaeological clues scattered through history. We know, for example, that both the Chinese and the Egyptians were making and drinking beer well over five thousand years ago. A four-thousand-year-old clay tablet, found in what was once Mesopotamia, shows that brewing was already a highly respected profession by that time. At New York's Metropolitan Museum of Art, an ancient Babylonian tablet lists a menu of beers including dark, pale, and red beers, beer with a head and beer without a head, and so on. In Israel, beer mugs dating back three thousand years have been discovered. There is even a four-thousand-year-old Assyrian tablet that claims beer was among the provisions on Noah's ark. We knew that Noah was no fool.

The Egyptians showed the ancient Greeks how to make beer, who in turn taught the early Romans, who spread the word about brewing, winemaking, and various culinary arts all over the Mediterranean area and as far away as Britain. Of course, Britain was never conducive to growing grapes in abundance, so naturally beer became the drink of choice for the ancient tribes, and eventually they would learn how to distill that beer into whiskey.

Those who think that brewing and beer drinking are strictly manly pursuits may be surprised to learn that throughout antiquity women were the brewmasters, both in royal circles (in ancient Egypt women brewers were also priestesses) and in the home, where beer making was considered part

of the household chores, along with cooking and raising the children. This remained true up until medieval times, when various trade guilds were established, and, in an act of supreme ingratitude, women were excluded. It was also during the Middle Ages that many of the household arts, such as brewing, cheese making, and winemaking, moved into the monasteries, where they remained and flourished until more enlightened times.

Knowledge of distilling came later than the discovery of fermentation, and, like so many other things, it is generally attributed to the ancient Egyptians, who initially used this technique not to make potable spirits, but rather to make perfumes and medicines. In time, of course, they discovered that by distilling the flavors and aromas of various plants, they could make some interesting beverages as well. The Arabs picked up where the Egyptians left off, but again it was perfume, not booze, that spurred them on, since alcohol was and is forbidden in the Muslim faith (ironically, the words *alcohol* and *alembic*, for the still in which it is made, both come from Arabic). In time, the Arabs took their show on the road to Spain, where they ruled and flourished for almost eight hundred years. From Spain, the knowledge of distillation naturally traveled to the rest of Europe, again mostly carried by monks and traveling pilgrims, notably to France, Holland, Scandinavia, and the British Isles. During the dark times of the Middle Ages, distillation moved into the monasteries, along with so many other food arts that involved flavor, artisanal methodology, and pleasure. The monks kept the art alive, developing along the way many unique spirits and liqueurs. With the dawn of the Renaissance, the stage was set for the modern era of alcoholic spirits as we know them today.

It was at the request of a distiller that Louis Pasteur, the great French chemist and bacteriologist, began his groundbreaking research. He started by studying fermentation, the process by which all alcoholic beverages are made. In an amazing bit of coincidence, he discovered pasteurization.

FERMENTATION AND DISTILLATION

In order to make spirits, you first need a fermented liquid, such as wine or beer. Virtually any food in a liquid form containing sugars (or starches that can be converted into sugar) can be fermented, and most will do so naturally if conditions are right. Although similar to the process of making sourdough bread, today fermentation is a controlled and highly precise science. To this liquid, yeast is added—either naturally or by the human hand—and then the action begins. The yeast cells feed off the sugars, devouring them and converting them into ethanol (ethyl alcohol) and carbon dioxide. This conversion is a violent process and makes the liquid appear to be boiling. In fact, the word *fermentation* comes from the Latin word *fervere*, meaning "to boil," an apt description of the party taking place within the vat. When the process is completed, you're left with a fermented brew—wine if grapes or other fruit is used, or beer when grain is the medium. Other raw materials used for making alcohol include potatoes and beets (some vodkas), sugarcane sap (rum), and the juice from the agave plant (tequila). But these fermented liquids are not yet spirits, and in fact, this is only the starting point where distilled spirits are concerned. Once the liquids are fully fermented, they're ready to go to the still to be transformed into spirits.

In theory, distillation is really a very simple process, and the basic procedure has changed little from ancient times. What makes it all possible is the fact that alcohol boils at a much lower temperature than water (173 degrees Fahrenheit versus 212 degrees Fahrenheit, respectively). The alcoholic liquid, such as beer or wine, is heated to a high enough temperature to boil the alcohol, converting it to vapors. These vapors rise up to the top of the still, where they're trapped and allowed to cool back into a liquid form, whereupon they are collected and siphoned off.

Although the theory is simple, in practice it's an exacting art that requires great skill, patience, and experience on the part of the distiller to produce truly fine spirits. The first liquid to come out of the still (the *heads*) and the last (the *tails*) are considered undesirable because they contain too many impurities, or *congeners*, that would adversely affect the final spirit. Therefore, only the heart of the distillation is generally used (the heads and tails are usually redistilled). Knowing exactly when to start collecting the spirit and when to stop is a skill that only comes from a great deal of experience.

The original still, and the type that was used exclusively for centuries, is called a "pot still," or "alembic still." They are made of copper and shaped like a big onion, similar to the famous domes on the buildings around Red Square in Moscow. This simple design performs distillation at its most basic; that is, heating the liquid so that the vapors rise up into a slender tube that then drops and spirals down, cooling the newly distilled spirit as it goes. This type of still, albeit more complicated, continues to be used today for many fine spirits, including Scotch single-malts, bourbon, Cognac, and others.

The second type of still, a *continuous still* or *column still* is sometimes referred to as a "Coffey still," named for the man who patented the invention based on a slightly earlier model developed by a Scotsman, Robert Stein. It involves two cylindrical columns that contain a series of steam-heated tubes and cooling plates, the purpose of which is to distill large quantities at a time without having to redistill, as is necessary with a pot still. As the liquid passes through the various chambers of the still, it's heated, cooled, and heated again, resulting in a much purer distillate. This type of still is used for making many brands of vodka, gin, and neutral grain spirits used for blending. A variation of this type of still is used to make Armagnac, the great French brandy (more about this in the section on brandy).

It's important to note that all newly distilled spirits, even those normally associated with color such as whiskey and brandy, are completely clear. Any coloration of the spirit is due either to long aging in wood barrels—typically oak—from the addition of caramel coloring, or both. The finest spirits take on their lovely amber hue exclusively from sitting in barrels for many months or years.

 On the eve of America's Prohibition, many towns were so convinced that drinking alcohol was the source of virtually all crime that they actually sold their jails.

STORING SPIRITS

Although spirits are far less perishable than fermented beverages such as wine and beer, they're not immortal and won't benefit from sitting around aging like some wines. In every case, spirits are ready to consume when put into bottles. Rest assured that the distillers have done all the aging— usually in wooden barrels—that the spirit will ever require. Spirits, again unlike wine, should be stored standing up straight, especially if they have corks. The alcohol in spirits will destroy the cork if left in contact long enough, which in turn would not benefit the spirit. Generally, spirits that have been opened will remain perfectly good for at least a year providing they have been kept closed and away from heat and direct light. Keep unopened spirits in a cool, dark place, such as a wine cellar. If you use speed pourers at home, either wrap them with plastic wrap when not in use or save the bottle caps and replace them between cocktail sessions.

PARTY POOPERS

Ever since the discovery of distilled spirits, certain groups have aligned themselves staunchly against the very idea of drinking, and saloons in general, deriding them as sinful, slothful, and downright ungodly, and these groups have tried to outlaw alcohol and its consumption. As we stumble forth into the twenty-first century, hopefully a more enlightened time, many of the taboos have been lifted, and today bars are viewed in a much healthier light. More and more, scientific evidence suggests that alcohol is beneficial in moderation, something we have believed all along. Studies show that one or two drinks a day can be beneficial in relieving stress, helping to ward off such things as heart disease and hypertension. In fact, studies indicate that people who consume at least one drink of alcoholic spirits a day live longer and enjoy better health.

The early temperance movement had to contend with the seemingly contradictory allusions to alcohol in the Bible, such as Jesus drinking wine (they insisted he really drank grape juice). Their solution was to hire a scholar to rewrite the Bible to remove any offending references to alcohol.

The ongoing debate over the healthfulness of alcohol consumption reminds us of an old joke about a professor trying to make his point about the evils of alcohol. He stood before his class with two glass beakers, one filled with water and one with whiskey. He dropped an earthworm into the water, whereupon it swam around a bit, settled on the bottom, and then was scooped out by the professor.

"Now look what happens when I drop him in the whiskey," he exclaimed. As the worm hit the whiskey, it reacted with a shock, convulsed violently, and died. "Now, what can we learn from this experiment?" queried the old professor.

A smart-aleck student in the back spoke up, "If you drink whiskey, you won't have worms!"

 Among the punishments for drinking thought to be just by U.S. Prohibitionists were the following: concentration camps in the Aleutian Islands, various methods of torture, branding, sterilization, exclusion from any and all churches, and being hung by the tongue from an airplane and flown over the country. Some were more succinct and simply suggested the offending person should be executed along with all progeny into the fourth generation.

EVERYTHING IN MODERATION

We believe that alcohol is an enjoyable and healthful part of everyday life, but only when consumed responsibly and in moderation. The purpose of drinking should be to enjoy oneself, socialize, take the edge off the day, and experience the myriad flavors of fine spirits and fermented beverages—not to get drunk. The following are some tips on enjoying alcohol in moderation:

- Know your limit. Most people can consume one drink per hour without feeling intoxicated. Others, however, feel wobbly after one cocktail. Experiment in safe surroundings with people you trust.

- Eat food while you drink. Eating, especially high protein foods like meat, nuts, and cheese, will help slow down the absorption of alcohol into your bloodstream.

- Sip your drink. You'll enjoy it more and be less likely to overdo it.

- Don't play drinking games or engage in chugging contests. They are the playground of the stupid. If you want to be naughty, play strip poker instead.

- Keep active. You'll tend to drink less and you'll be more aware of the effects of the alcohol than you would be sitting on a sofa all evening.

- Be careful when drinking punches and fruity drinks that disguise the taste of the alcohol. They go down very easily and you'll be drunk before you realize what's happening.

- If you're at a party for several hours, alternate drinks with an occasional nonalcoholic beverage. You'll be less likely to get wasted and you'll feel better the next morning.

- Don't let anyone coerce you into drinking beyond your limit, or into drinking at all. If you're uncomfortable not drinking at a party or bar, ask for juice or soda over ice in a highball glass and no one will know the difference. Hey, it works for lap dancers.

- Never mix drugs and alcohol. If you're taking medication, make sure you know how it reacts with alcohol. Sometimes even small amounts of one or the other can cause ill effects.

- Do we need to say this? Don't drink and drive. You endanger not only yourself, but also others, if you drive under the influence. Remember what Dean Martin said, "If you drink, don't drive. Don't even putt."

The body actually produces its own alcohol. A small amount of alcohol is generated every day in the intestines from naturally occurring bacterial flora that ferment. In other words, everyone has some alcohol in their bloodstream at all times, whether they drink or not.

HOW ALCOHOL AFFECTS THE BODY

Despite the huge amount of enjoyment one can derive from drinking spirits, it's important to remember that alcohol is a drug, and a rather powerful one at that. And while our inclusion of a section on how alcohol is processed in the body may be akin to describing the process of digestion in a cookbook, we feel it's better to understand how alcohol works in order to better safeguard against excess. Like anything that's consumed, alcohol goes down the esophagus, spends some time in the stomach, and finally goes to the small intestine. Along the way, a small amount of alcohol is absorbed into the bloodstream through mucous membranes, but mostly alcohol gets into the bloodstream by passing through the walls of the small intestine. Since alcohol is water soluble and is greatly diluted by the body's own fluids, the blood carries it quickly through the body, where it's absorbed into various body tissues in direct proportion to that area's water content. A small amount of alcohol, actually in proportion to the amount in the bloodstream, transfers from the blood into the lungs, where it's expelled through the breath. Because the amount is a reflection of the amount in the blood, a person's blood alcohol concentration (BAC) can be determined with a breath analyzer. No amount of chewing gum, mouthwash, or other breath fresheners will prevent the breath analyzer from detecting the amount of alcohol in the breath.

Modern scientific research tells us that moderate drinkers outlive the teetotalers. In a remarkable bit of foresightedness, one Colonial-era insurance company charged people who didn't drink an extra 10 percent in premiums over those who did drink.

Although minute amounts of alcohol avoid metabolism and are eliminated unaltered through the breath, perspiration, and urine, most alcohol is metabolized in the liver. The liver detoxifies the alcohol by means of oxidation and removes it from the blood, thereby preventing it from accumulating and potentially destroying cells and organs. However, the liver can only metabolize a certain amount of alcohol every hour, the amount depending on several factors, such as the size and weight of the individual and the amount of food eaten. Generally speaking, after consuming a standard drink (defined as 12 ounces of wine, 6 ounces of beer, or 1.5 ounces of 80-proof distilled spirits), one's BAC peaks in about 30 to 45 minutes. The most important thing to remember is that alcohol metabolizes more slowly than it is absorbed into the bloodstream. For the average person weighing about 150 pounds, the body can handle about one drink per hour without any noticeable signs of intoxication. There remains a common myth that drinking coffee will sober you up. The fact is only time will bring about sobriety, not black coffee, cold showers, or any other so-called "cures." A drunk person who drinks a lot of coffee will still be drunk; they'll just be wide awake.

overheard

To be intoxicated is to feel sophisticated but not be able to say it.
—Anon.

the
REALM
of the
SPIRITS

Why does gin taste like it does?

When first distilled, gin is exactly like vodka, a clear, relatively tasteless alcohol. Gin, however, is then infused with an assortment of botanical flavorings, most prominently juniper berry, that give it its distinctive flavor.

Was vodka originally made from potatoes, and is it still?

Vodka, like any alcohol, can be distilled from any fermentable carbohydrate, including potatoes, but is most often made from grain. Since vodka's genesis pre-dates the introduction of the potato to Europe from South America, it's a myth that it was first made from these edible tubers. Today, some vodka is made from potatoes, and no doubt several farmhouse versions exist, but the vast majority of vodkas are made from grain such as rye, barley, oats, or wheat.

Is it true that gin is more intoxicating than vodka?

Assuming the alcohol level is the same, the effect on the consumer would be the same.

If vodka is flavorless, why pay more for premium brands?

Although by law vodka is a flavorless alcohol, in fact different brands do have subtle but distinct differences in flavor as well as mouthfeel. The best way to judge is to taste them side by side.

Is flavored vodka a modern invention?

Various fruits, herbs, and other flavorings have been added to vodka for as long as there has been vodka.

GIN AND VODKA

The Workhorses of the Modern Bar

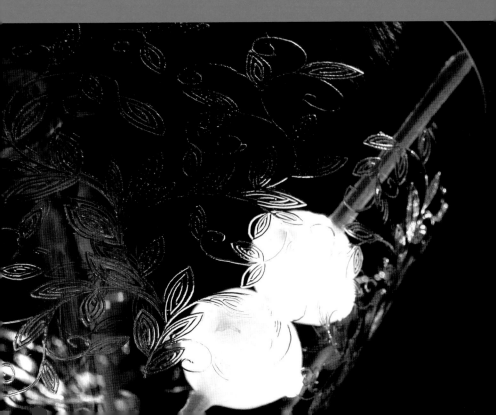

Although they originated in different parts of Europe at different times, gin and vodka are closely related in terms of the methods of production and their use at the bar. It has been said that gin is simply flavored vodka or, conversely, that vodka is gin with the flavor left out. This is unfair to both and yet there is some truth to the assertion. Both are clear distilled spirits made from fermented grain (except that vodka can be and sometimes is made from beets or potatoes) that require no aging and rarely see the inside of a wood cask. While their histories are quite different, at the modern bar they are virtually two sides of the same coin. They are traditionally the most asked for spirits at the bar, not by themselves but in the form of countless cocktails, the names of which could fill the annals of a cocktail hall of fame. The Martini lifts these two liquors to exalted status, and although purists maintain that gin is the only acceptable spirit in a Martini, in our experience they are asked for equally often.

Gin and vodka are virtually interchangeable in many of the most popular cocktails, including the aforementioned Martini, as well as the Gimlet and Collins. (Tom Collins is made with gin; with vodka it is sometimes called a Joe Collins, but usually simply called a Vodka collins.) They are also interchangeable in simple highballs mixed with tonic or soda. While gin is associated with a longer list of cocktails and is arguably the superior of the two spirits, vodka is not far behind in the cocktail count (with more being added all the time) and has actually become more popular at the bar, especially among younger drinkers who want a kick to their drink but don't really like the taste of alcohol. In the end, both are noble spirits with long and interesting pedigrees whose place at the bar is assured.

GIN

Though it has lost much of its popularity in the past several decades (losing ground especially to vodka), gin is still the quintessential bar spirit and figures into many of the world's most famous cocktails. Gin is most famous for its role in the Martini, although again, the Martini today is more often made with vodka, much to the horror of Martini aficionados. Still, the United States remains the single largest market for gin in the world, including both imported brands and domestically made versions (although per capita, Spain is the largest consumer of gin—go figure). In reputation, gin has gone from being the scourge of the lower classes in England to its current image as an elegant, sophisticated, and slightly mysterious cocktail component. Gin drinkers are an unapologetic lot, and one assumes they like the taste of liquor, for no matter how gin is served, it manages to make itself known. Gin doesn't disappear beneath tonic, lime, or even a healthy dose of Campari and sweet vermouth, as in a classic Negroni cocktail. It almost seems that, like connoisseurs of fine whiskies, those who drink gin are accorded a bit more respect at the bar.

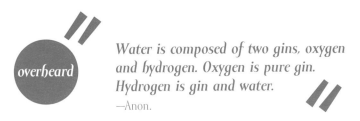

overheard

Water is composed of two gins, oxygen and hydrogen. Oxygen is pure gin. Hydrogen is gin and water.
—Anon.

Gin is a clear, grain-based distillate flavored most prevalently with juniper berry, among several other herbs, spices, roots, and seeds, known collectively as "botanicals." These can include, but are not restricted to, coriander seeds, caraway seeds, aniseed, orange peel, cassia bark, licorice, cardamom, cinnamon, fennel, ginger, almonds, orrisroot, and angelica root. Less common flavorings include saffron in the Old Raj brand and cucumber in Hendrick's, both brands from Scotland. Distillers avidly guard their recipes, but juniper berries are always used, and in fact, it is the bluish green berries of the evergreen juniper shrub that originally gave gin its name, from the French *genièvre*, and the Dutch *genever*, ultimately shortened by the British to gin.

Gin was invented in Holland, and although its earliest history is a bit obscure, it is generally believed that a seventeenth-century physician and scholar, Franciscus de la Boe (aka Dr. Sylvius), in the Dutch university town Leyden, was the first to manufacture gin by combining juniper and distilled grain spirits in an attempt to cure kidney and bladder ailments. He named it "Essense of Genièvre," and although it did little or nothing to help one's kidneys or bladder, it tasted great. It was soon discovered by British soldiers stationed on the continent, who brought it back to England.

When Dutch Protestant William III married Mary II to become king of England, he took advantage of his position to get back at the Catholic French by imposing restrictive duties on French wines and brandies. This embargo greatly increased the demand for the less expensive English gin, and by the early eighteenth century, things in jolly old England were completely out of hand. London, especially in the slums of the poor and middle classes, was like Bourbon Street during Mardi Gras, an all-out drunken orgy wherein people even fed gin to their neglected infants and many literally died in the streets. This sad and shady period in English history survives in William Hogarth's famous engraving "Gin Lane," a drawing that shows the unbridled debauchery and ghostly pallor of the masses consumed with cheap, poisonous gin.

An attempt at prohibiting the supply of gin proved about as successful as prohibition ever is (in other words, not at all), but things eventually quieted down and more reasonable laws were put into effect that governed how and by whom gin was distilled, ensuring at least that it was properly made and held to some standards of hygiene and quality. Finally, after Aeneas Coffey patented the continuous still (see Fermentation and Distillation), a lighter, purer, and no doubt better-tasting gin was developed. And because the purer gin didn't need to be masked by sweetness, a drier gin came to be the preferred style. By the dawn of the twentieth century, London dry gin was a standard everywhere in the world where the Union Jack waved.

In America, our own relationship with gin has been equally tempestuous. What whiskey was to the Wild West, and what absinthe was to the bohemian artists of the Moulin Rouge, gin was to the speakeasies during our own Prohibition in the 1920s. Gin gained popularity no doubt because it could be made quickly and cheaply (hmm, Gin Lane all over again) without the prolonged barrel aging required for whiskey, something that would have been impractical for bootleggers who were always on the move. For all of gin's presumed elegance and sophistication today, it was once reviled as a wicked, violence-inducing, troublemaker of a beverage. Some people still believe that one gets drunker and crazier on gin than any other spirit and refuse to keep it in their home bars. For others though, it is as essential to modern life as cell phones and iPods, most often in the form of a Martini, easily the most famous of all cocktails.

Owing much to the vast reaching of the British Empire up until the Second World War, gin has become a staple of cocktail bars throughout the world. The standard is what is known as "London dry gin," although several other types still exist. The major factors in determining the quality of any gin are as follows:

- The quality and purity of the base grain spirit.

- The quality of water used for both fermenting the grain and diluting the gin to drinkable levels.

- The type of distillation employed.

- The quality and variety of the flavoring agents (botanicals) used by the distiller. The actual lists of ingredients are closely kept secrets in the gin-making trade.

LONDON DRY GIN

Although it was originally a geographical distinction, the term, "London dry" today refers to the style of gin. It can actually be made anywhere, although many of the best and most famous examples are still made in the United Kingdom, but not necessarily in London. It is hands down the most popular style of gin in the world, and in almost any recipe calling for gin, it is implied that London dry is the gin to use unless specifically stated otherwise. By far, the majority of the gin sold in the United States is made either here or in England. Any gin labeled "London dry" must by law possess a strong juniper flavor, and the juniper and other botanicals must be

"Bathtub gin" was so called because the cheap gin (a mixture of alcohol, glycerin, and juniper juice) produced during Prohibition was mixed in very large bottles, or carboys, too tall to fill in the kitchen sink, and so were routinely filled in the bathtub.

infused through the distillation process rather than simply added, as is the case with compound gins (wherein extracts from juniper and other botanicals are simply added to neutral grain spirits).

The standard method for making any London dry gin is as follows:

1. Grain is cooked and fermented, typically corn, malted barley, and small amounts of some other grain. The solids are strained away, leaving a fermented liquid known as "beer" or "wort."

2. The wort is distilled in a continuous still.

3. The infusion of the botanicals occurs in one of two ways: either the spirit is redistilled in a continuous still with the botanicals suspended high up in the chamber so that the rising vapors pass through them; or the spirit and the botanicals are distilled once more together in a traditional pot still, thus bringing about the infusion of the flavors.

London dry gin, exemplified by such brands as Beefeater, Gilbey's, Tanqueray, and Bombay, is a light-bodied, very pure alcohol with the unmistakable essence of juniper, coriander seed, and other flavorings. It is the gin of choice for cocktails, from Martinis to a gin and tonic, as its light, clean style blends effortlessly with the other components of the drink.

PLYMOUTH GIN

The English port city of Plymouth has its own unique style of gin, and it is no doubt this spirit's relationship to the sea that made it the official gin of the British navy. With the addition of lime and quinine water (tonic), it has been keeping scurvy and malaria at bay on Her Majesty's ships for generations. Unlike London dry, Plymouth gin must be made within the city of Plymouth, although as of this writing there is only one distiller of Plymouth gin remaining, Coates & Co., a firm that also controls the rights to the name. Plymouth gin is fuller-bodied than London dry and very aromatic. It is the preferred spirit for a Pink Gin (gin and Angostura bitters), in part because British sailors kept Angostura bitters in their medicine kits, and partly because the robust character of Plymouth gin stands up better to the strong bitters.

HOLLAND, DUTCH, OR GENEVER GIN

The birthplace of gin still produces a style of gin that is full-bodied and distilled in traditional pot stills. It begins life in much the same way as whiskey, the wort resulting from the fermentation of malted grain mash. There are two main styles:

Oude ("old"), a very aromatic, bold, straw-colored liquor that has a faint sweetness; and *Jonge* ("young"), which is lighter, clearer, and drier.

Holland gin is thought by many to be too strong in flavor for use in cocktails and is best enjoyed sipped neat or over ice. Today, Holland-type gin is also made in Belgium and Germany. It is the only type of gin that is routinely aged in oak casks, sometimes for as long as three years.

VODKA

For hundreds of years, vodka has been the drink of choice throughout Eastern Europe, Scandinavia, and, most famously, Russia. Since the 1950s it has steadily gained popularity in the United States as well, even eclipsing gin as the preferred base for a Martini. By nature, and certainly by any legal definition, vodka is a colorless, odorless, and flavorless spirit that blends easily with all sorts of mixers, including fresh fruit juices, soft drinks, and liqueurs. Or so the Bureau of Alcohol, Firearms, and Tobacco would have us believe. Vodka's image of neutrality is misleading, for although it is indeed without color, premium vodkas from around the world come in an astonishing array of textures and flavors, though admittedly the differences can be subtle. In spite of the efforts put forth by the world's distillers to imbue their vodkas with distinctive character, vodka's ability to enliven a cocktail without actually tasting like alcohol, along with some very good marketing, has popularized it among younger drinkers and made it America's favorite spirit.

Similar to the debate between Ireland and Scotland over who invented whiskey, Poland and Russia have been sparring for generations over the true provenance of their beloved vodka (*wodka* in Poland, but pronounced the same), with the Poles even claiming that the Russians had no word for it until the Poles gave it to them. To an outsider it seems like a silly enough argument, considering that the earliest forms of vodka were no doubt quite crude, nothing anyone would want to lay claim to. However deep runs this strain of nationalistic pride, the most likely answer to the argument is that they both began making the distilled spirit at about the same time, give or take a few decades. Vodka has been documented as being made as early as the twelfth century, but no matter which country first made it, the Russians surely deserve the credit for perfecting it. Many of the early experiments with distilling, redistilling, and filtering vodka were done in Russia, mostly on the estates of the czars.

The name *vodka* comes from the Russian *zhizennia voda*, or "water of life," a term that was no doubt applied to any alcoholic spirit at the time, especially since they all would have been made originally for medicinal applications. *Vodka* is the diminutive form, "little water," which may have

been used to set vodka apart from spirits in general once they had finessed the recipe a bit, or it may simply reflect the fondness in the Russian vernacular for familiarizing names.

A popular myth that still finds its way into print is that vodka was originally made from potatoes. Though potato-based vodkas have been and continue to be made, potatoes were unknown in Europe until well into the sixteenth century. Then and now, most vodkas come from grain (usually rye, corn, barley, or wheat), although anything that can produce a fermentable mash will do, such as potatoes, beets, or molasses. Today, most vodkas are made in continuous stills, which can achieve the level of purity desired in vodka, and are distilled to a very high proof, after which they are filtered through charcoal or quartz to remove any impurities. Some vodkas, particularly in Europe, are still made with pot stills, in which case the spirit is distilled two, three, or even four times. Many distillers and connoisseurs feel that, although more laborious, the pot still method leaves more of the character of the grain in the final spirit.

Among the things we owe to the Russian revolution in 1917—such as *Doctor Zhivago* and a plethora of Cold War spy novels—we might just count vodka's presence in America. At one time, the czar banned the manufacturing of vodka for the same reasons the English tried to control gin. As we know, prohibition never works, and countless illegal stills were set up all over the country. By the time this was all beginning to resolve, the revolution came, and although vodka was once again in favor, all the distilleries were owned by the state. As a result, the Smirnoffs took their show on the road, ending up in the United States, where the firm Heublein bought the rights to the name and began to make vodka domestically.

If you're a bird, don't drink and fly. A report from Sweden says that thousands of waxwing birds became, well, drunk, when they pigged out on berries that had fermented. Approximately fifty of them lost their lives when they flew into closed windows. The report didn't say whether any fighting or pregnancies resulted from the avian orgy.

Despite some terrific marketing (involving a salesman in South Carolina who called it "Smirnoff White Whiskey"), World War II intervened and interrupted vodka's rise to prominence. However, some even more terrific marketing in the 1950s, again by Smirnoff, vaulted vodka to its place as America's premier spirit. "It leaves you breathless," uttered by a succession of celebrities of the day, was the provocative ad line that implied not only a titillating good time, but also no telltale alcohol on the breath back at the office. Of course, the latter is a fallacy, as is the belief that drinking vodka won't lead to a hangover because of the lack of impurities. Although many people think vodka is a safer bet for that reason, a hangover is a symptom of alcohol withdrawal, and immoderate drinking of any alcoholic beverage can bring one on.

Flavored vodkas have become very popular, leading one to think they are a modern concoction. However, the concept of adding flavorings to vodka goes back to their earliest days. The relative neutrality of vodka makes it a perfect vehicle for added flavors. In the beginning, various flavors such as honey, herbs, and spices were added to disguise the undoubtedly horrible-tasting crude spirit. Pepper-flavored vodka, or *pertsovka*, is taken directly from Peter the Great's habit of adding hot chiles to his vodka. Other flavorings, such as lemon, orange, and other fruits, were common throughout the nineteenth century in Russia. "Hunter's style" vodka (*okhotnichya*) is a flavor extravaganza, containing lemon peel, ginger, clove, coffee, anise, other spices, sugar, and sweet wine.

Vodka is the base spirit for many of our most cherished and time-honored drinks, like the Screwdriver, Vodka Collins, and Bloody Mary, and modern cocktails, like the Lemon Drop and Cosmopolitan. And, as already mentioned, it is increasingly the spirit called for in Martinis. Vodka mixes well with almost anything or can be served straight up or on the rocks. It is also the perfect partner for caviar and smoked salmon, especially when served ice cold from the freezer. In fact, premium vodka, frozen to attain a viscous, syrupy consistency and served in tiny tasting glasses or sherry glasses, is a lovely aperitif all on its own or with a twist of lemon.

What are the ingredients used to make whiskey?
Whiskey is essentially distilled beer, or fermented grains such as barley, oats, rye, wheat, and corn.

What is the difference between bourbon and Scotch?
Both are whiskies, but Scotch is made in Scotland from malted barley. It is characterized by a distinctive smoky flavor. Bourbon is American whiskey and is made predominantly from corn. It generally has a much sweeter flavor than its Scottish counterpart, with hints of vanilla.

What is malt?
Malt is grain (typically barley) that is moistened and allowed to partially germinate, or sprout. For Scotch single-malts, the malted grain is dried over peat fires, lending a smoky flavor.

What is the difference between Scotch whisky and Irish whiskey?
The most substantial difference is that in Ireland the malted grains never come into contact with smoke, so Irish whiskey lacks that smoky character found in Scotch.

What is a single-malt Scotch?
It's a Scotch malt whisky from one single distillery, as opposed to blended Scotch, which is a mix of one or more single-malts with a more neutral grain whisky.

What are blended American whiskies?
These are straight whiskey blended with neutral grain spirits.

WHISKEY AND WHISKY
Legends in the Mist

Whiskey is a grain-based distillate that derives its amber brown color and a significant amount of its flavor from long aging in oak barrels. It is easily one of the world's oldest and most revered spirits, and its place in Western culture and lore is legendary. Its early history though, is as foggy as the moors of Ireland and Scotland, the two countries that were the first to make whiskey (which country was first depends on whether you ask an Irish distiller or a Scottish one). Most experts believe it was introduced to the British Isles by monks out spreading the Gospel sometime in the first millennium A.D. These tippling friars would have called it *aqua vitae*, Latin for "water of life," which translated to the Gaelic as *uisge beatha*, or *usky* for short, a term that the English would eventually turn into *whisky* (the spelling used by the Scots and Canadians, whereas *whiskey* is used by the Irish and most American distillers). Thanks in part to the expansion of the British Empire as well as to the spirit's almost mythic status in Hollywood cinema, whiskey's fame spread to every corner of the globe, and today whiskey production has emerged in countries as far-flung as Japan, Australia, Spain, Germany, India, Korea, and Brazil. The big four producers, however, constituting most of the discussion henceforth, are Scotland, Ireland, Canada, and the United States.

Whiskey is made from grain, water, and yeast, distilled, and then aged in oak barrels for anywhere from a month to several decades. The various whiskies of the world can be light-years apart in terms of flavor, character, and body. There are several influencing factors that determine the outcome of any whiskey, as follows:

- The kind of grain used and how that grain is processed. The cereals used for whiskey are almost always corn, rye, barley, wheat, oats, or a combination of two or more of these.

- The quality of the water source. Traditionally, all the notable areas of whiskey production have been near pristine springs or other natural sources of water.

- The type of still employed for distillation (see Fermentation and Distillation).

- The type of wood used for aging (for example, French oak versus American oak and how the barrels are prepared (for example, charring the interior or using barrels in which some other alcoholic liquid has previously been aged).

- The length of time the whiskey is aged.

- Where it is aged, especially in terms of its proximity to the sea.

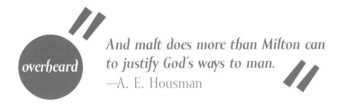

And malt does more than Milton can to justify God's ways to man.
—A. E. Housman

At its most basic, whiskey is made by first cooking the grain in water and then adding yeast to induce the initial fermentation. At this stage the resulting liquid is essentially beer, and is often referred to as such by distillers. However, it is in the distilling of this beer and subsequent barrel aging that it becomes whiskey (when first distilled it is as clear as vodka, and indeed, bears little difference). There are several distinct types of whiskey, and each of the four major whiskey-producing countries has their own unique methods and ingredients.

SCOTLAND

Scotch whisky has a style and flavor unique among whiskies, and many consider it to be the king of spirits, rivaling even the great French brandies as the paragon of civilized drinking. Scotch whisky, of course, refers to any whisky made in Scotland, and by law it must be distilled there and aged a minimum of four years. But, as any avid Scotch drinker will tell you, this spirit is defined as much by its distinctive character as it is by its place of origin, although the two clearly go hand in hand. Despite the enormous popularity in recent decades of single-malt varieties, Scotch drinkers are still basically divided into two camps: those who prefer blended Scotch whiskies, and those for whom nothing will suffice but pure single-malts that can range from elegant, subtly smoky whiskies to full-throttle, take-the-chrome-off-your-bumper spirits that are without question an acquired taste.

Like all whiskies, those from Scotland are based on grain, and in the case of single-malts that grain is always barley (grain whiskies typically use wheat and/or corn). The process by which the barley is readied for the still, however, is what sets Scotch apart from almost all other whiskies. There are several unique factors that determine the ultimate quality of Scotch whiskies, especially in the category of single-malts:

• The quality of water used for germinating the grain, initial fermentation, and reducing the alcoholic strength; distillers take great pride in the quality of their water and it is perhaps the single most important element in the process.

• The quality and type of peat used to dry the malt.

• The type of oak barrels used for aging.

• The distillery's proximity to the sea. The bracing salt sea air of the North Atlantic lends a tangy saline quality to the whisky during the aging period, especially evident in the Islay malts.

• The length of time the whisky spends aging in wood.

According to the *Oxford American Dictionary*, the word *Scotch* is an archaic term for Scottish, meaning "of or relating to Scotland." It is no longer used in that context, however, and is generally disliked by the Scottish people. Therefore, a person from Scotland is either Scottish, a Scot, a Scotsman, a Scotswoman, or, well, a person from Scotland. The term *Scotch* remains only in certain fixed, traditional phrases, such as Scotch broth (a Scottish soup made from meat broth, barley, and vegetables) and, of course, Scotch whisky. If you want a Scotch while in Scotland, simply ask for whisky or name your brand.

Although all whiskies are made in fundamentally the same way, the extra steps involved in Scotch whisky production are key to its singular nature. The process is as follows:

1. The barley is moistened with water and allowed to partially germinate (similar to making sprouts at home or in those grade-school botanical experiments involving seeds and wet paper towels).

2. After the grain has begun to sprout, it's dried in a special kiln over fires fueled by peat harvested from the nearby moors. This process releases the malt sugars that are held inside the barley.

3. The grain is cooked in water, yeast is added, and fermentation begins, wherein the yeast consumes the malt sugars and converts them to alcohol. The solids are removed and discarded.

4. At this point, the beerlike liquid (typically known as "wort" or "wash") is sent to the still. Malt whiskies are distilled at least twice and sometimes three times in old-fashioned pot stills, while grain whiskies are distilled in column stills (see Fermentation and Distillation).

5. Once the distillation is complete, the "baby whisky" (a colorless spirit that's approximately 70 percent alcohol by volume, or ABV) is pumped into oak barrels, slightly diluted to about 60 percent ABV, and then placed in the aging rooms to begin the long, slow maturation period.

The barrel aging of any brown spirit (such as whisky, brandy, and dark rums) is crucial to the character and flavor of the final product, and malt whiskies from Scotland are no exception. Scottish distillers prefer barrels that have been previously used to age other alcoholic beverages such as bourbon, sherry, port, Madeira, and, more recently, the red wines of Bordeaux and the white wines of Sauternes. They even joke that those beverages exist only to prepare the barrels for the making of Scotch whisky (bourbon makers are not amused). By law, whisky in Scotland is aged a minimum of four years, although five to ten years is fairly standard, and some, like fine wine, can age much longer. It is the responsibility of the master distiller to determine at what age the whisky has reached its peak of maturity.

In spite of the prestige of, and slavish devotion to, single-malts, connoisseurs actually owe much to the blended Scotch whisky industry—an industry that, in terms of volume, completely dwarfs the malted whisky side of the business and, indeed, has kept the production of malted whisky viable. Master distillers in Scotland use dozens of single-malt whiskies, usually from several different distilleries, in combination with grain whiskies to make their blends. This is an exacting process whereby they strive for consistent flavor and character from batch to batch. The quantities of a single-malt are typically very small, but together they act as building blocks to achieve the desired end. The market for blended Scotch whisky, both at home and abroad, essentially finances the production of single-malts. Despite the often hefty price for the upper echelon of whiskies in Scotland, the individual distilleries could not survive on these single-malts alone.

WHISKY-PRODUCING REGIONS OF SCOTLAND

It's tempting to make generalizations about the nature of the whiskies of each region, but in fact, except for the smallest island regions (which only have one or two distilleries), each produces plenty of variation in style and taste.

Highlands   This is the largest and most famous of the whisky regions of Scotland, within which are several subregions, including the North, East, and West Highlands and the islands of Orkney, Arran, Jura, Mull, and Skye. Some of these regions, such as the islands of Orkney and Skye, have only one or two distilleries, while other areas contain clusters of distilleries, such as the Northern Highlands area from Inverness up. There is no single style of Highland malt whisky, except to say that they are generally known for being well-balanced, elegant, and rather complex. They can range from delicate, almost flowery spirits, such as Oban, to full-bodied, complex whiskies like Dalmore and Glenmorangie.

Speyside   This region is contained within the Highland region but has come to be regarded on its own as an autonomous region. Located in the northeast corner, roughly between Aberdeen and Inverness, but including neither, this area is sometimes called the "Golden Triangle" because of the number of distilleries found therein. Although named for the river Spey, there are actually many rivers that traverse the area, many of which

what's in a name?

No one has yet published a definitive explanation for why the Scots spell it *whisky* while the Irish spell it *whiskey*. Both forms derive from the same Gaelic root, *uisge beatha*, and since nobody seems to know for sure who first made the beverage as we know it, the Scots or the Irish, there is little to go on. Our theory is that due to the rivalry between the two neighboring countries, the word is spelled differently simply to distinguish their wares, one from the other. As for other countries' choice of spelling, it seems fairly straightforward: The Irish were the first to engage in any significant whiskey-making in the United States, and therefore *whiskey* is used most commonly, although a few bourbon makers (such as Maker's Mark, Old Forester, and Early Times) use *whisky*, presumably as a nod to their Scottish ancestry. Canada and other British Commonwealth countries opt for the Scottish spelling, as does Japan, where Scotch whisky is revered and emulated.

evoke the great whisky brands themselves, such as the rivers Livet and Fiddich. Speyside is home to some of the biggest and most revered names in Scotch, such as Macallan, Glenlivet, and Glenfiddich. The much-sought-after single-malts of this region tend to be mellow and elegant but defy any one stylistic category.

Islay   The island region of Islay (pronounced EYE-lay), off the southwest coast of Scotland, easily produces the most robust and peatiest single-malts. The whiskies of this area are the most definable, heavily influenced as they are by both the heavy layer of peat that covers the island (and permeates the water) and the proximity of the sea. Not for the faint of heart, these whiskies, such as Bowmore, Lagavulin, Laphroaig, and Caol Ila, are highly regarded by Scotch drinkers.

Campbeltown   Geographically part of the Highlands, this once highly productive coal area lies at the southern tip of the peninsula Mull of Kintyre. Rich in barley fields and the all-important peat, Campbeltown once boasted over thirty distilleries and was a major whisky-making hub. Today there are only two distilleries remaining, Springbank and Glen Scotia, but Campbeltown nevertheless retains its own regional classification.

Lowlands   Home of Scotland's beloved poet Robert Burns and the country's two largest cities, Glasgow and Edinburgh, this southernmost region creates lighter, less peaty whiskies, many of which are used to blend with the more robust whiskies of the Highlands.

In general, the body of a whiskey is either light or heavy in direct proportion to the size of the grain used to make the mash. A large grain such as corn results in a lighter-bodied spirit, while whiskies made from rye, a much smaller grain, tend to be heavier.

SCOTCH WHISKY TERMS

Single-malt   Each single-malt whisky uses malted barley and hails from a single distillery, although not necessarily from the same cask, nor even the same vintage. To achieve consistency, some distillers mix in different vintages, in which case the youngest whisky is the age listed on the bottle. As long as the vintages are from the same distillery, however, the whisky is still considered a single-malt. When malt whiskies from different distilleries are blended, it is known as "vatted malt" because distilleries generally blend their whiskies in huge vats. This distinction is seldom indicated on the label, which instead simply describes the contents as "malt" or "pure malt." Any malt whisky not specifically labeled as single-malt can be assumed to be a vatted malt.

Scotch grain whisky   Mostly used for making blends, these are rarely bottled straight and therefore this term is seldom seen on labels. They are made primarily from wheat or corn, usually with a small amount of barley and barley malt that has not been dried over peat. Grain whisky accounts for the vast majority of whisky made in Scotland.

Blended whisky   A blend of grain and malted whisky. There can be as many as forty whiskies—both malt and grain—used in blends, with the amount of malt anywhere from 5 to 70 percent. Deluxe blends, such as Chivas Regal, are those with the highest percentage of malted whisky.

Peat   A highly compacted, compostlike substance made up of grasses and heather that is harvested from the moors along the coastline. Peat has been used for centuries as fuel for cooking and heating throughout Scotland and Ireland. In the making of Scotch whisky, it is the earthy, pungent aroma of the peat that is responsible for the whisky's distinctive smoky taste.

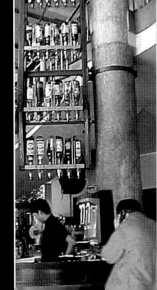

IRELAND

Much to the chagrin of their Scottish neighbors, Ireland claims to have been the first country in the United Kingdom to learn the craft of distilling, and thus would be the birthplace of whiskey. Popular legend even has it that it was Saint Patrick himself who brought the knowledge and skills of distilling to the Emerald Isle. At the end of the nineteenth century, Ireland had upwards of two thousand distilleries (albeit many of them were illicit makers of poteen, the Irish equivalent of moonshine), with as many as four hundred Irish brands for sale in America. Today there are a scant three, one in Northern Ireland (Bushmills, the world's oldest distillery) and two in the Republic of Ireland.

Several setbacks contributed to Ireland's decline from its position as the premier whiskey-making country. Ironically, it was an Irishman, Aeneas Coffey, who patented the continuous still (based on a model invented by a Scot named Robert Stein) that would make it possible for Scotland to create their lighter, blended whiskies that appealed to modern tastes. Just as these less expensive blends began to conquer the lucrative U.K. market, civil war and the battle for independence in Ireland effectively closed England as a viable marketplace, leaving the United States as the single largest customer for Irish whiskey. Unfortunately, a few years later America's Prohibition was decreed by the Volstead Act of 1920, the reactionary amendment that dealt such a crushing blow to America's own distilleries, breweries, and wineries, and all but sounded the death knell for the Irish whiskey industry.

Irish whiskies are made much in the same way as the malted whiskies of Scotland, with the notable exception that the malted barley is dried in kilns in which the grain never comes into contact with smoke. Hence, they lack the smoky, peaty character loved by Scotch drinkers. Whiskey in Ireland is usually blended, either a blend of malts or malts combined with other grain whiskies, but is also bottled as pure single-malt. Irish whiskey is typically sweeter and fuller-bodied than its Scottish counterpart.

UNITED STATES

America's love of whiskey extends back to colonial times, and next to rum was most likely the first spirit to be produced here, especially after the British cut off supplies of rum during the Revolution. The birth of our domestic whiskey industry was due to the many Scottish and Irish immigrants who did what they had done back home, that is, set up and run stills to turn part of their grain harvest into whiskey. At first, they used the same grains they would have used in the Old Country, rye and barley. In time, however, as these distillers moved west with the expansion of the fledgling country, they found the perfect setting in Kentucky to make their spirits. They had fertile land for the growing of grain, pristine spring water and plenty of it, and forests of oak trees from which to make barrels for the all important aging of the spirits. Corn quickly supplanted barley as the base grain in this new land of Kentucky and a new whiskey was born, one that has virtually become synonymous with American whiskey, bourbon.

Bourbon   Although originally named for Bourbon County, Kentucky, the name "bourbon" today refers to the ingredients used and the method of production, and although the majority is still made in the state of Kentucky, technically bourbon can be made anywhere in the United States. Bourbon must be made primarily from corn—no less than 51 percent and not more than 80 percent (if more than 80 percent, it's called "corn whiskey"). The remaining grain consists of malted barley and some other grain, typically rye or wheat. Law also stipulates that bourbon be aged a minimum of two years in oak barrels, although most of them are aged much longer. The typical taste of bourbon is sweet from the corn, with vanilla-laden overtones contributed by the oak. Bourbon whiskey is most often enjoyed straight or mixed with water or soda, but it is also the base spirit for a number of classic American cocktails, notably the Manhattan, the Old-Fashioned, and the Mint Julep.

Abraham Lincoln had bourbon in his blood. Born in Bourbon County, Kentucky, his father worked occasionally at a whiskey distillery located at Knob Creek, for which a modern, small-batch brand of bourbon is named today. Long before he became president, according to the *Bourbon County Reader*, Abe himself had a liquor license and operated several taverns.

what's in a name?

Bourbon County, Kentucky, for which all bourbon is named, was established during the American War of Independence in the late eighteenth century. To honor our French allies, it was named for the reigning French royal family of the day, the Bourbons. In the early days of Kentucky's whiskey trade, Ohio River docks in Bourbon County were the point of departure for all the liquor produced in the region. From there the whiskey was sent down the Ohio to the Mississippi and on to New Orleans. All the barrels would have been stamped with the port of origin, or "Bourbon," and thus the singular spirit came to be known throughout the world. Ironically, Bourbon county never repealed the Prohibition Act and continues to forbid consumption of alcohol to this day.

Tennessee whiskey   *Tanasie*, as the Cherokee called it, was first settled by Irish distillers fleeing the whiskey taxes levied in the East. They found abundant land for growing grain and plenty of fresh water in which to ferment that grain. Tennessee whiskey (an official designation only since 1941) differs from bourbon in only two respects: corn is not required to be the dominant grain, although it always is; and after the whiskey is aged, it must be passed through approximately ten feet of sugar maple charcoal to filter out the last remaining impurities. This process, known as "charcoal mellowing," "leaching," or the "Lincoln County Process," results in a mild, smooth whiskey. There are only two distilleries left in Tennessee, but they are especially notable in that one of them, Jack Daniel's, is routinely listed among the thirty or so best-selling whiskies in the world. The other, George Dickel, is also a venerable old distillery of American spirits. Booker Noe, the master distiller for Jack Daniel's and great-grandson of Jack, once commented on the differences between the whiskies produced by the two by saying, "Same church, different pew."

Rye whiskey   Once very popular in America, rye whiskey seemed to lose its luster among consumers until very recently. Rye is made today exactly like bourbon, except that rye replaces the corn. It is a uniquely American invention, and is generally more assertive and spicier than bourbon. Happily, rye whiskey is making a decided comeback, mostly in the form of small-batch or single-barrel versions. Such brands as the seductive Black Maple Rye, Michter's Single Barrel Rye (dates back to 1753), and Old Potrero Rye from Anchor Brewing have been eliciting praise from critics and consumers alike.

AMERICAN WHISKEY TERMS

Blended whiskey   These consist of two or more straight whiskies mixed with neutral grain spirits for reasons of consistency and economy. They must contain at least 20 percent straight whiskey.

Sour mash   A method by which a portion of the mash, or grain mixture, from the previous batch of whiskey is added along with the yeast to begin fermentation, similar to what bakers do when making sourdough bread. The "setback," or "stillage," as it is variously called, passes on some of the character of the whiskey while also helping to keep the yeast under control. Virtually all straight whiskies in the United States are now made in this way.

Straight whiskey   This is unblended American whiskey. It must be distilled from at least 51 percent of any one grain with the remainder made up of other grains, and no neutral grain spirits are added. Virtually all straight bourbons, ryes, and Tennessee whiskies are made by the sour mash method as well.

The first Kentucky whiskey is said to have been made in 1789 by a Baptist minister, the Reverend Elijah Craig (1743–1808). Craig also was the first distiller to blend corn, barley, and rye for his mash, and the first to use charred oak barrels for aging his whiskies. The Heaven Hill Distillery in Bardstown, Kentucky, honored the right reverend by naming one of its whiskies after him.

In 1964, the U.S. Congress declared that bourbon was such a distinctive product that it should forever after be regarded as the official spirit of the United States. Take that Prohibitionists!

overheard

Whiskey smells like a mouse's nest, but the contrary is not really true.
—Anon.

CANADA

Ironically, the decade-long prohibition on alcohol in the United States, one that all but decimated the Irish and American spirit industries, turned out to be a great boon to the Canadian whisky business. In order to supplement all the cheaply made U.S. whiskey and gin, or perhaps simply to avoid having to drink them, large quantities of Canadian whisky were slipped over the border into the United States. The blended Canadian whiskies were much lighter in body than bourbon or rye, and consequently precipitated America's taste for lighter whiskies, epitomized by such brands as Canadian Club and Seagram's V.O. It wasn't until the 1980s that Americans began to turn back to the more pronounced flavors of straight bourbon whiskey and single-malt Scotch. Nevertheless, Canadian whisky still outsells American whiskey in the United States.

Canadian whiskies are mostly blended whiskies, and although the government of Canada doesn't stipulate exactly how these whiskies are made, they have mandated that Canadian whisky be made from cereal grains. Rye, corn, and barley are mostly used, although Canadian distillers are very closemouthed about their formulas. Canadian whiskies are also required to be aged in wood casks for at least three years.

Canadian distillers prefer oak barrels that have been used to age bourbon, sherry, brandy, or other spirits. Lesser brands have also been known to add small quantities of fortified wines and other flavorings to enhance their product, and since there are no regulations saying they can't, it remains a trade secret. The proof is in the pudding though, and the better brands are smooth, likable, and satisfying whiskies. Canadian whiskies are generally perfect for mixing, either in cocktails or in classic highballs. They can also be enjoyed straight or on the rocks, especially the deluxe blends like Crown Royal and other reserve blends. Some producers in Canada are beginning to make whiskies with more individual character, including small-batch and single-barrel versions, so it will be interesting to watch the progress of our northern neighbors in the years to come.

What is tequila?

Tequila is a spirit distilled from the juice obtained from the heart of the agave plant (*Agave tequilana Weber azul*), a large, spiky-leaved plant in the lily family related to the century plant.

What is the difference between tequila and mezcal?

All tequila is mezcal, but not all mezcal is tequila. Tequila must be grown and distilled within specifically delineated areas in the state of Jalisco and must be made from at least 51 percent blue agave (the finest are 100 percent). Mezcal can be made anywhere in Mexico from any type of agave (usually one of eight varieties out of the possible four hundred known).

Is it true that tequila often has a worm in the bottle? And is the worm really hallucinogenic?

No. Mezcal is the spirit famous, or infamous, for having a worm in the bottle (the maguey "worm" is actually the larva of a moth that naturally breeds in the agave plant). In reality, this is rarely done anymore, and the presence of a worm should in no way be regarded as a sign of quality. And no, the worm is no more hallucinogenic than the mezcal itself.

Does mezcal come from the same plant as mescaline, the hallucinogenic drug?

No. The confusion results from the anglicized spelling of mezcal. *Mescal* with an *s* is a cactus from which the hallucinogen mescaline is extracted. It is not related to the agave plant, which is not a true cactus.

TEQUILA AND MEZCAL

The Whiskies of Mexico

Tequila and its cousin mezcal are distillates made from the fermented juice, or sap, of the agave, a unique plant native to Mexico. They are in a sense the whiskies of Mexico, and like whiskey, they are at home both as sipping liquors and as the base for some classic cocktails. Although the first shipments of tequila came to the United States as early as 1873 (from the Sauza distillery, quickly followed by a shipment from the Jose Cuervo company), tequila first really became known to us gringos during Prohibition in the 1920s. Just as thirsty patrons in the East relied on illicit shipments of whisky from Canada and rum from the Caribbean, imbibers out West, particularly the Hollywood crowd, looked to Mexico to satisfy their thirst for alcohol. But it wasn't until the 1950s that tequila became widely known throughout the United States, mostly in the form of the now-ubiquitous Margarita cocktail. Since then, tequila has steadily gained in popularity, and as our taste for more full-flavored spirits—single-malt Scotch and small-batch bourbons, for example—has increased, finely crafted tequilas have become popular in bars and restaurants across the country. Most sources agree that the Margarita is the most popular cocktail in America, both at home and in bars, an assertion we are inclined to believe, or at least ponder over a cold Margarita.

What is the difference between tequila and mezcal? As tequila marketers are so fond of saying, all tequila is mezcal, but not all mezcal is tequila. Tequila is generally regarded as the superior of the two, but it's increasingly difficult to distinguish them by quality alone, since there are currently mezcal producers, such as Del Maguey, making first-rate spirits. And conversely, there is plenty of indifferently made tequila. An analogy can be made that tequila is to mezcal what Cognac is to Armagnac. Mezcal is rougher and a bit untamed, but it can be very good and sometimes outstanding. Ultimately, however, what separates tequila from mezcal is where it is made, the methods of production, and the type of agave used.

TEQUILA AND AGAVE AZUL

The agave plant is a spiky-leaved relative of the century plant in the lily family, not a cactus as many believe. It grows throughout Mexico, and locals there have been drinking the fermented sap from the agave, known as *pulque*, since ancient times. When the Spanish conquistadores arrived in the fifteenth century, they brought with them the knowledge of distillation and, once their supply of European spirits ran low, quickly set about distilling pulque. The result was often less than satisfying, but in time it was discovered that one variety, the blue agave, worked best and produced a very good spirit indeed. They also figured out that if the stalk, or heart, of the agave (where the sap is located) was first cooked, it concentrated the natural sugars and made for a better-tasting drink. Thus tequila was born.

By law, in order to qualify as tequila, the blue agave must be grown, processed, and distilled in one of several areas in the state of Jalisco in southwestern Mexico. The best tequilas, and really the only ones worth considering, are made exclusively from 100 percent blue agave, or *Agave tequilana Weber azul*. (Dr. Weber, for whom the plant is named, was the one who brought to light the superiority of the blue agave for distillation into a spirit.) We say "the best" because the law only stipulates that tequila be made with 51 percent blue agave, and producers often use various types of sugar to make up the difference. Tequilas not made from 100 percent blue agave are known as *mixtos*. Always select tequila clearly labeled "100% Blue Agave" and with a registration number that begins with the letters NOM (Norma Oficial Mexicana). Think of it as a Good Housekeeping Seal of Approval for tequila. Any tequila that doesn't have those two specifications on the label can be assumed to be a mixto.

what's in a name?

Tequila is named for the town in Jalisco where production is centered, which in turn is named for the Tiquilas, a tribe who inhabited the area before they were bullied out, and no doubt destroyed, by the conquistadores. Mezcal, probably the older of the two spirits, derives its name from *metl*, the Aztec word for the agave plant itself. The name *pulque*, for the fermented sap that's the base for both spirits, is a corruption of the Aztec word *octili poliqhui*.

Unlike faster-growing grains, sugarcane, or even grapes used for other distilled spirits, the agave plant must grow almost a decade before it can be harvested. When the plant reaches sexual maturity, it starts to grow a flower in the middle. The grower cuts off the flower stalk, forcing all the plant's resources back down into the heart, or core, of the plant. This core, known as a *piña*, looks rather like a pineapple on steroids (*piña* is Spanish for "pineapple"). They weigh anywhere from 25 to 125 pounds, with some known to have tipped the scales at upwards of 200 pounds. The length of time it takes to grow agave adds to the uniqueness of tequila, but has also led to its undoing. Because of the enormous popularity of Mexican spirits in the United States and elsewhere, tequila producers are experiencing a shortage of agave. In other words, they are running out of their raw material. This shortage is further complicated by the Mexican law that stipulates tequila must be aged in the province in which it is grown and made. One result of this has been efforts to grow agave in other places, notably South Africa. So far, the quality of the South African spirits has been less than inspiring, and the Mexican government has used legal means to keep the interlopers from co-opting the name *tequila*. Nevertheless, the market demand for quality tequila and mezcal will surely prompt others to try to replicate the spirit, and it is also likely that Mexico will consider relaxing regulations on where in their country agave can be grown in order to satisfy a thirsty public.

TEQUILA VARIETIES

For many tequila drinkers in the United States, there are two kinds of tequila, white and gold, with the gold varieties considered the more full flavored and upscale due to aging. In truth, much of what is sold as "gold" tequila is aged only slightly or not at all, relying instead on the addition of a small amount of aged tequila or caramel coloring for color and flavor. The aging of tequila is a curious thing. As with whiskey and brandy, aging in wood adds flavor and color to the spirit. However, tequila differs in that it can only withstand a limited amount of aging. Up to four years in wood can be very beneficial, but more than that and tequila begins to deteriorate, diminishing in quality rather than improving with each passing month. The following are the most common forms of tequila found in the United States.

Blanco (white)   Also known as "plata," "sterling," or "silver" tequila, blanco refers to clear, unaged tequila that is typically bottled right after being distilled. It can be either 100% blue agave or a mixto. Naturally, this type of tequila is less expensive because it hasn't been aged, but it shouldn't be thought of as inferior since many 100 percent blue agave blancos are excellent tequilas, either for sipping neat or for mixing in cocktails.

Reposado   In Spanish, *reposado* means "rested," and as the name suggests, this is tequila that has only spent a short time in oak barrels. The law stipulates that reposados must be aged no less than sixty days and no more than one year. Reposados can be either 100 percent blue agave or mixtos.

Añejo (old, or aged)   These tequilas are aged up to four years, resulting in a lovely amber color from the wood, as well as sweet, caramel-like flavors. If they are 100 percent blue agave, the law insists they be aged a full four years to be labeled añejo. The barrels of choice are those previously used to age Kentucky bourbon. This level of tequila is highly regulated, and once the barrels are filled, they're sealed by the government to ensure there are no shenanigans.

Research from around the world shows that countries with higher alcohol consumption rates have fewer drinking problems than countries with relatively low consumption rates.

MEZCAL

Mezcal has a much broader definition than tequila. Upwards of four hundred varieties of agave have been cataloged, and Mezcal can legally be made from any of them; however, it's typically made from one of eight varieties, and most often from either espadin agave or maguey agave. There are few laws governing the production of mezcal, and much of it is still made in old-fashioned, usually homemade, ovens. Due in part to the shortage of blue agave, more attention is being paid to small-village mezcals. The aforementioned Del Maguey produces several outstanding examples of traditional mezcal, all labeled according to the village in which they're made, and one that's made from 100 percent tobala, a wild mountain maguey. At $20 a shot, the price is more likely to take your breath away than the spirit—it's very smooth and delicious, and can put to rest any prejudice against mezcal.

What is rum made from?

Rum is distilled either from molasses left over from processing sugar or, in some cases, directly from the fermented juice, or sap, of the sugarcane.

If rum is made from sugar, are all rums sweet?

No. In fact, some of them are quite dry, and some, when aged in wood, taste almost like whiskey. Many rums do, however, retain a hint of sweetness, especially if aged in wood, and some are lush with sweetness, especially the dark, aged varieties.

Does all rum come from the Caribbean?

Rum can be made anywhere sugarcane is grown, although most of the best and most famous brands are produced among the island nations strung across the Caribbean Sea, as well as several areas in Central and South America. Cachaça is a type of rum made in Brazil. Furthermore, some are made in one place, at the source of the sugarcane, and then aged elsewhere, such as in England and Scotland. Cadenhead's rum is aged near the sea in Scotland and takes on a noticeable saline quality.

RUM
Adventure on the High Seas

We owe the existence of rum as much to Columbus and the European craving for sweets as to the seemingly universal thirst for alcohol. Rum, one of the oldest distilled spirits in the world, is made from sugarcane or, more accurately, from the molasses left over from processing sugarcane (though it can also be made directly from the sap or juice). Today, some form of rum is made virtually everywhere that sugarcane is grown, including Australia (Inner Circle traditional pot still rum). Some of the hottest brands are being made in Venezuela, whence we get examples like Pampero Anniversario and Santa Teresa 1796 Solera. Nevertheless, the best and most famous brands, as well as most of the stories and legends connected with rum, come from the island nations strung across the Caribbean Sea. In fact, one brand from Puerto Rico, Bacardi, is the largest producer of rum in the world., and white rum in general gives vodka a run for its money as the preferred spirit the world over. Increasingly though, rum producers are catering to an up-and-coming market that favors bolder flavors, and therefore the styles of rum are fuller, more complex spirits made for sipping straight and for a bevy of enticing cocktails.

To really understand rum, however, one must first understand sugarcane and how it is processed to make sugar. Sugarcane (*Saccharum officinarum*), a tall, tropical grass whose hollow stalk is filled with pulp containing sweet sap, probably originated in what is now Indonesia. It made its circuitous route to the Caribbean via Asia, India, the Middle East, and North Africa. Portuguese and Spanish traders eventually planted it in the Azores and the Canary Islands. It was from the latter, his last port of call before reaching the West Indies, that Columbus took sugarcane cuttings on his second voyage to the New World. Sugarcane thrived in the Caribbean soil and climate and quickly became a major cash crop. At that time, sugar was still a fairly exotic and costly food, much desired in Europe, and consequently hundreds of sugar plantations emerged throughout the various Caribbean colonies in order to meet the demand.

The process for making sugar is as follows:

1. The sugarcane is crushed between huge rollers to release the sap inside (this sap is composed of about 18 percent sugar).

2. The sap is boiled, evaporating the water, further breaking down the sugars, and causing them to crystallize and clump together.

3. Centrifugal force is used to separate the sugar crystals from the remaining juice, which is by now a sticky syrup, or molasses (from the Portuguese *melaço*, in turn from the Latin *mellacium*, based on *mel*, meaning "honey").

Work is the curse of the drinking classes.
—Oscar Wilde

Molasses still contains a large amount of sugar, so much so that it won't ferment until it has been thinned out with water. Early on, plantation owners and those who ran the sugar mills discovered that, if left out in the sun for a few days, the rehydrated molasses would ferment. Very quickly the clever colonists turned what was essentially waste into a cash crop even more lucrative than sugar by distilling the fermented sweet sludge into rum. It then became quite common to locate a distillery next to the sugar refinery on the plantation, with the molasses simply carted next door to be distilled. As a result, not only did a by-product become a viable commodity, but since rum was much less perishable than molasses, it was easier to transport on long ocean voyages. It was, as they say today, a win-win situation.

The origin of the name *rum* (*ron* in Spanish, *rhum* in French) is quite obscure and is the subject of great debate. Some have speculated that it comes from the Latin genus name for sugarcane, *Saccharum*. We think that's lame. It's doubtful that the first people making rum would have known the Latin name, and it certainly would not have been in common use. Others have theorized that it derives from *rumbullion*, an archaic word that refers to the often unruly behavior brought on by overconsumption of rum. Another possible source is the Malay word *brum*, for a kind of liquor made from sugarcane. We prefer another, much simpler, theory: For many years rum was the official quaff of the British navy, with each sailor guaranteed a daily ration. The British expression *rum*, an adjective meaning "a jolly good thing," dates from the seventeenth century. We can just hear those solid, seafaring English lads describing their daily grog as being "a rum drink indeed."

The history of rum is a colorful one indeed, and humanity's tenuous relationship with the spirit can be summed up by an old Jamaican saying: "God caused men to raise themselves up onto their feet; rum sees to it that they fall over again."

Or, as Captain Flint repeatedly sings in Robert Louis Stevenson's *Treasure Island*,

> *"Fifteen men on the dead man's chest*
> *Yo-ho-ho, and a bottle of rum!*
> *Drink and the devil had done for the rest*
> *Yo-ho-ho, and a bottle of rum!"*

In general, the process by which molasses is turned to rum is as follows:

1. The molasses is reboiled, resulting in a low-grade sugar.

2. Other ingredients are then added: water, yeast, and often *skimming* (the foam that rises to the surface and is skimmed off when the original sap is boiled) and *dunder* (the residual sediment left over in the still from the previous distilling, similar to the sour mash method in whiskey production).

3. The molasses mixture is left to ferment for anywhere from twenty-four hours to several weeks, depending on the style of rum desired (the slower the fermentation, the stronger the bouquet).

4. The fermented brew is distilled, usually twice, in either a pot still or a column still (see Fermentation and Distillation).

5. Most rums come out of the still at around 130 to 180 proof, and they require some amount of aging for the various acids, esters, and alcohol to bind together and mellow out.

Generally, making rum in a pot still produces rich, full-bodied spirits, and a column still produces light-bodied rums due to their better separation of undesirable elements. Rum is generally divided into four categories, light-bodied, medium-bodied, full-bodied, and aromatic. There are also rums marked "añejo," which simply means "aged"; these are usually a tawny color with a mellower flavor. By law, rum must declare its country of origin on the label, and although there are no regulations governing the style of each country, most rum-producing countries do have a distinctive, recognizable style. Throughout the latter half of the twentieth century, as lighter spirits like vodka came to be preferred, so too did the lighter rums, such as Bacardi, rise in popularity. Today, as tastes in spirits are beginning to lean more to the fuller-bodied, full-flavored styles like small-batch bourbons and single-malt Scotch, the darker, fuller-bodied rums are gaining in popularity as sipping liquors. Here's a rundown of some of the major rum-producing locales and styles.

> **overheard**
> *Reminds me of my safari in Africa. Somebody forgot the corkscrew and for several days we had to live on nothing but food and water.*
> —W. C. Fields

Puerto Rico   This prosperous U.S. commonwealth, sometimes referred to as America's fifty-first state, may have been the first spot in the Caribbean where rum was made. Ponce de Leon, the island's first governor, established a distillery there soon after he arrived in 1508, and today Puerto Rico is the world's largest producer of rum. Puerto Rican rums are made from molasses in continuous stills, and most of them are light-bodied and dry, as exemplified by the island's chief ambassador, Bacardi white rum. They are made in a manner similar to sour mash whiskies, in other words, with the skimming and dunder added into the molasses before fermentation, and are typically aged in oak casks, either charred or not. On the other end of the rum spectrum is the elegant Ron de Barrilito from the Edmundo B. Fernandez Distillery. Made in relatively small batches, these rums are excellent for sipping or for making more flavorful cocktails. Adding to the diversity of Ruerto Rican rums is the producer Serrales, maker of the hugely popular Captain Morgan spiced rums, a concept that goes back to the earliest days of rum drinking. Puerto Rican law allows for the addition of sherry or Cognac to enhance flavor and aroma. Puerto Rican rums are aged at basically three different levels: one year, resulting in light, dry rums, which are filtered to remove any trace of color from the wood; three years, during which time the rum takes on an amber to golden hue (caramel color is added to enhance the color); and six years and over, *vieux* (old) or liqueur rums.

For most people, the history of the rum trade is one of colorful pirates and swashbuckling adventures on the high seas, but there is a seamier side to rum's early history. In the eighteenth century, distilleries were established in New England to feed the thirst for rum, which was then the most popular spirit in the young colonies. (Whiskey would later supplant rum as settlers began moving away from the coast and found grain easier to come by than molasses.) Thus molasses would be shipped up to New England, where it was distilled into rum. Some of the rum in turn was shipped to the Gold Coast of Africa and traded to the local chieftains for slaves, who were then sent to the Caribbean in exchange for more molasses, and so on. This infamous "Slave Triangle" was a reprehensible episode in our history, made even worse when you realize that slaves from Africa were needed because the European conquerors had decimated most of the indigenous peoples throughout the Caribbean, who, strangely enough, didn't want to be enslaved.

Virgin Islands   Most of the rums made here are almost identical to those from Puerto Rico. They have strayed from that profile, however, with such rums as Cruzan Single Barrel Estate.

Demerara (Guyana)   These are very dark rums with a high proof (usually 151 proof), and yet they're medium-bodied. Demerara rum was for several hundred years the official bracer of the British navy, and it is the original spirit called for in a Zombie cocktail.

Jamaica   Known for being dark and mellow, Jamaican rum is fermented for a full three weeks and is naturally fermented, meaning there is no added yeast and no mash held over from the previous batch. It is double distilled in pot stills and aged in oak casks for a minimum of 5 years. Caramel color is routinely added.

Martinique and Haiti   Rums from these countries are distilled directly from the sugarcane juice, rather than molasses. They are concentrated by boiling down the fermented juice to about a third of its original bulk and distilled in pot stills. Aged in oak casks, they are generally medium-bodied, excellent for sipping neat. One of the most famous of Haitian rums, and one of the best rums on the market, is from the Barbancourt distillery.

Aguardiente de caña   This generally refers to rums from Central and South America, the most famous of which is cachaça (see below). One of our favorites is Flor de Caña, a wonderfully dry golden rum from Nicaragua.

Cachaça   Is it a brandy or a rum? Cachaça (also *caxaca, caxa, chacha*; pronounced kah-SHAH-sah) is usually referred to as brandy in Brazil, its country of origin, because it's distilled directly from fermented sugarcane

juice and not molasses. However, since we define brandies as being made from fruit (and particularly grapes), we have included cachaça here as a rum. Cachaça is made by first allowing the sugarcane juice to ferment naturally in large copper or wood containers for three weeks. It is then boiled down to a third of its original bulk and distilled in either a pot still or a continuous still. Cachaça is best known to most *norte americanos* as the spirit base for the increasingly popular cocktail, Caipirinha, a delightful blend of cachaça, lime, and sugar that is essentially the national drink of Brazil.

Batavia arak   This is a curious rumlike spirit, and one that has been known by Europeans since the seventeenth century. Arak, or arrack, is a general term that refers to all sorts of vegetable-based distillates made throughout the Orient. This particular one, made in the town of Batavia in Java, is made by submerging Javanese red rice cakes into molasses and allowing the mixture to ferment naturally. The mix is distilled in pot stills and put up in oak casks to age for three years. It is then shipped to Holland, where it is aged for another six years before being blended and bottled. Mostly supplanted by rum in Europe, arak is mainly still used to make various grogs and punches.

File this under divine drinking. In 1116 B.C.E., an imperial edict in China decreed that drinking alcohol in moderation was required by heaven. In the West, the picture of heaven imagined by pre-Christian Anglo-Saxons was that of a place where one could visit with other deceased people and enjoy alcoholic beverages. Certainly something to look forward to.

DISTILLED FACTS

What is brandy and how is it made?

Generally speaking, brandy is distilled wine. Brandy made from fruit other than grapes is called either "fruit brandy" or "eau-de-vie." Wine or fermented fruit is distilled either in traditional pot stills (as Cognac is) or in continuous stills (as Armagnac is). Brandies distilled from wine are aged for a number of years in oak barrels, from which they derive their color and a significant amount of flavor. Typically, fruit brandies are not aged in wood or at all and remain clear.

What is the difference between Cognac and Armagnac?

Both are named for the regions in which the grapes are grown and the brandy is made. The differences are many: Cognac is double distilled in pot stills, Armagnac in continuous stills. Cognac is almost never a vintage brandy, and Armagnac often is. Cognac is aged in oak barrels, first new wood and then used barrels; the Armagnacais prefer black oak barrels, but increasingly they use Cognac-style barrels. Armagnac has also been around almost two hundred years longer than Cognac.

What are grappa and marc?

They are *pomace brandies,* or brandies that instead of being made directly from wine are made from the leftovers from the winemaking process—the skins, seeds, stems, and pulp—which are then reconstituted and distilled. Grappa is Italian and marc is French. They are rarely aged and almost never see the inside of a barrel and are therefore clear distillates.

What is Calvados?

It is apple brandy from the Normandy region of France. It is distilled twice in pot stills and aged in oak barrels.

BRANDY
Fruit of the Vine . . . and Tree

Anywhere wine is made in any significant quantity, it's likely that brandy, often called the "soul of wine," is also produced. Likewise, in places throughout Europe and the United States where other types of fruit are grown in abundance, you will probably find an assortment of fruit brandies, or eaux-de-vie. Brandy is made from fermented fruit juice, typically from grapes, that is then distilled either in traditional pot stills or in modern continuous stills. It can be bottled almost straight from the still or aged. Brandies were likely the world's first distilled spirits, and the ancient Egyptians and Arabs no doubt distilled grape-based wines in their alchemic search for medicines and perfumes. Brandy can effectively be divided into three groups, as follows.

Brandy or grape-based brandy   These are the most common, and the brandies of France—notably Cognac and Armagnac—are the most famous of all and have set the standard by which all other brandies are judged. Distilled wine is aged for several years in oak casks that, as with whiskey, impart color and a certain amount of flavor. Not surprisingly, the major brandy-producing countries are also known for their wine, especially France, Italy, Spain, and the United States. All of these countries make excellent brandies, although those of France are the most famous.

Fruit brandy or eau-de-vie   Any fruit can be fermented and then distilled into fruit brandy. Among the fruits commonly distilled are apples, cherries, raspberries, plums, pears, figs, and more. There are various methods for making fruit brandy, but they share a common trait in that they are rarely aged in wood and therefore remain clear. The best fruit brandies are distilled in such a way as to retain the essence of the fruit.

Pomace brandies   These were originally a by-product of the wine-making process, a way of not letting anything from the harvest go to waste. Pomace brandies—known as "grappa" in Italy and "marc" (pronounced MAHR) in France—are made from the pulp, skins, and stems left after the grapes were pressed and the juice drained away. This residue is then diluted, some sugar is usually added, and the whole thing is distilled. Grappa and marc are rarely aged in wood, and like eau-de-vie (or any brandy when it is first made), they are generally as clear as when they came out of the still. Despite their waste-not-want-not genesis, many grappas and marcs made today are highly refined spirits that can fetch steep prices and are greatly sought after.

Brandy, especially wine-based brandy, has a long and illustrious history at the bar. In addition to being what many consider the ultimate ending to a great meal, brandy can also be enjoyed as an aperitif, either on the rocks, in a tall drink with soda or tonic, or in a number of cocktails, like the Horse's Neck, Stinger, Brandy Alexander, and, of course, the Sidecar, which is essentially a brandy sour and has become a favorite drink across the country. Arguably, the three most famous brandies, and the ones used most often at the bar, are all from France—Cognac, Armagnac, and one made from apples, Calvados. Most brandies made throughout the world emulate these styles, especially that of Cognac.

COGNAC

The brandies of Cognac have an illustrious heritage and a sterling pedigree as one of the world's finest spirits. They are famous throughout the world and are sold virtually everywhere on the planet—from four-star restaurants to skid-row liquor stores—with a price range to match. To many consumers, the terms *brandy* and *Cognac* are practically synonymous. In fact, one writer pointed out that, next to Paris, the town of Cognac is probably the most famous place-name in all of France, even though most people who know the term don't know it's a place at all. Cognac in general

In direct contrast to our own phobias related to alcohol consumption, no government health warnings are allowed on any wine imported into any country in the European Union (for the geographically impaired, that means Austria, Finland, Germany, Greece, Ireland, Italy, Luxembourg, the Netherlands, Portugal, France, Sweden, and the United Kingdom).

has a character that sets it apart from all other brandies, one that is indelibly linked to the land, the grapes, and the methods of production.

In order for a brandy to legally be labeled Cognac, the grapes must be grown and distilled within the designated Cognac area, one that strides two *départements* (administrative regions, kind of like our states), both of which take their name from the river Charente, which dissects the region: Charente-Maritime is on the Atlantic coast, and Charente lies directly inland to the east. The two principle towns of the region—especially as they relate to the business of Cognac—Jarnac and Cognac itself—are both situated on the Charente. The river played a major role in Cognac's rise to fame since access to the shipping lanes facilitated transporting the brandy around the world quickly and easily.

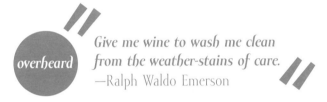

> Give me wine to wash me clean
> from the weather-stains of care.
> —Ralph Waldo Emerson

overheard

The Cognac region is divided further into six growing areas that fan out in almost concentric circles from the town of Cognac: Grande Champagne, Petites Champagne (no relation to the famous sparkling wine of the same name, but stemming from the same Latin word, *campagna*, meaning "countryside" or "open fields"), Borderies, Fins Bois, Bons Bois, and Bois Ordinaires (meaning "fine woods," "good woods," and "ordinary woods," respectively). Ironically, the latter three are not woods anymore at all— the trees were harvested long ago for barrels to age the spirits. The finest Cognac comes from the first two areas along with yet another designation, Fine Champagne, indicating a blend of grapes from Grande Champagne and Petites Champagne, with at least 50 percent of the grapes coming from Grande Champagne. The diversity of the region's climates and soil give rise to the different growing zones, and the unique nature of the Cognac region as a whole ultimately sets Cognac apart from all other brandies.

The grapes used to make Cognac produce very undistinguished wines that are thin and very acidic, qualities that have proven to be perfect for making fine brandy, since the acid adds structure to the brandy. The dominant grape is Ugni Blanc, which for some reason is called Saint-Émilion in the Cognac region (no relation to the Bordeaux wine district of the same name), followed by Colombard and Folle Blanche. There are five lesser varieties allowed by law, but the total of those grapes cannot exceed 10 percent of the grapes used.

Cognac is always distilled twice in a traditional copper pot still known as an *alambic charentais*, heated with gas. It was discovered early on that the grapes of the Cognac region only needed two distillations to be palatable, whereas those from other regions needed more, resulting in the loss of any semblance of the fruit. The first distillation, known as *brouillis*, is a cloudy liquid that's about 30 percent alcohol. The second distillation is called *la bonne chauffe*, or "the good heating," and results in a clear liquid closer to 70 percent alcohol (140 proof), or about twice the ultimate bottle strength. The skills of the master distiller are paramount in the making of Cognac, for it is knowing when to make the cut (*la coupe*) between the heads (the first liquid to emerge from the still) and the tails (the last to come out), separating out the heart (*la coeur*), that results in great brandy. The heads and tails of the distillation can be too rough, with off flavors that would adversely affect the brandy. They are generally redistilled on their own for production of cheaper brandies. The brandy at this point is a colorless liquid that is rather harsh in flavor.

The newly distilled brandy is then set aside for aging in barrels made from oak from one of two forests, Limousin or Troncais. Typically, Cognac starts the aging process in new barrels for mellowing and for color; those deemed appropriate for long-term aging are usually transferred to used casks so the flavors from the wood don't become too intense, overwhelming the grape essence of the brandy. The aging rooms, or *chais*, and the barrel warehouses are mostly situated along the banks of the Charente, as they have been for centuries. Humidity is crucial in the aging of Cognac: too little and more water evaporates than spirit and the brandy will be too harsh; too much and the brandy will lack structure. The air near the river provides the perfect level of humidity for the brandy, allowing for a slow but steady evaporation of the liquid, or what is referred to by the Cognaçais as the "angel's share." By all accounts, the equivalent of some twenty million bottles of Cognac disappears into thin air each year, a phenomenon

some claim results in the longevity of the people who live in the region. As the brandies age in barrels, the wood and oxidation slowly transform and mellow them. When the brandy is ready to be bottled, distilled water or water and Cognac that have been aged together are added to the barrel to bring the alcohol level down to 40 percent or 80 proof, as stipulated by law.

Cognacs, like many fine wines and spirits, are blended. Buyers of Cognac depend on their brand to have consistent flavor and character from year to year and decade to decade. Cognacs can be aged for up to sixty years, after which it is believed the brandy begins to deteriorate rather than improve. The age for any Cognac rarely appears on the label. What you do see is a series of letters, such as VSOP, that are a kind of code for the age of the brandy inside. These designations merely indicate the age of the youngest brandy in the blend, although the average age of all the spirits in the bottle is far greater. The Cognac label designations can be interpreted as follows:

- VS (very superior), or three-star. The youngest brandy in bottles labeled thus must be at least two and a half years old. The actual age is usually between four and seven years.

- VSOP (very superior old pale), VO (very old), or Réserve. The youngest here is at least four and a half years, with the oldest aged five to fifteen years.

- XO (extra old), Napoléon, Vielle Réserve, or Hors d'Age. These terms indicate an age of at least six years, but in reality much more like twenty to forty years.

- Many Cognac houses have come up with their own classification terminology for their older brandies, such as Rare & Delicate, Très Belle (very beautiful), Vénérable, Réserve Ancestrale, Antique, and Triomphe, among others.

Prohibitionists, struggling with the Bible's proclivity for alcohol, rankled at this quote: "Use a little wine for thy stomach's sake" (1 Timothy 5:23). They explained it to their followers by saying it was advising people to rub alcohol on their tummies. It is said that those same followers repeatedly purchased the Brooklyn Bridge.

Cognac's success is owed in large part to a great location and a series of fortunate events. Due to the easily navigable river Charente, the area was known first as a distribution point for salt, but by the beginning of the seventeenth century Dutch trading companies were buying wine from the slopes above the town of Cognac to supply their ships or, more accurately, their sailors. The wine was thin and spoiled easily and therefore was fortified with distilled spirits, much like sherry or port. To preserve the wine even more, the savvy Dutch began to take the wine back to Holland and distill it into *brandewijn*, or "burnt wine," using a process they had no doubt learned from monks, who would have brought it from Spain. Eventually, they brought stills down to the source and set up distilleries in the Cognac area. The first real Cognac house, Augier, set up shop in the mid-seventeenth century, and the industry was born.

Today, over two hundred firms distill Cognac from more than 200,000 acres of vines throughout the six growing areas. The so-called "Big Four" producers—Martell, Hennessy, Courvoisier, and Rémy Martin—account for a whopping 90 percent of all Cognac sold, four-fifths of it sold outside of France. In fact, France is only the sixth-largest market for Cognac, where it is as likely to be consumed as a *fine a l'eau* (brandy with water) as it is after dinner in a snifter. Many things have happened in recent years to take some of the muscle out of the Cognac industry. For one thing, the governing body has been stubborn in their refusal to state an age—even an average age—on the labels, preferring instead the rather convoluted, confusing, and archaic system described above. Cognac also has stiff competition these days from other spirits like Scotch single-malts, which do state the age of the spirit. Also, the grains used for whiskey production, both here and abroad, are much cheaper than grapes, are easier to grow, and can be stored for longer periods of time, allowing for year-round distilling.

One happy result of the trials and tribulations of the Cognac industry has been that many small, individual producers, who would have normally sold their stocks to the larger firms for blending, have found themselves with overstocks of aged brandy and are now selling them under their own labels, in the process giving consumers a much broader choice in Cognac. Thus, we have seen the emergence of heretofore unknown houses like Delamain, Pierre Ferrand, Camus, Clos du Colombier, Maison Surrenne, Giboin, Dudognon, and Jean Fillioux among others.

ARMAGNAC

The rough-and-tumble cousin to Cognac, Armagnac actually pre-dates its famous rival by almost two centuries, and yet Cognac became renown throughout Europe and the American colonies while Armagnac was simply regarded as a regional oddity. That has changed dramatically, however, as consumers are waking up to the distinctive and powerful flavor and aroma of this heady spirit, which is proving especially popular with lovers of single-malt Scotch, small-batch bourbons, and aged tequilas and rums. If Cognac were Audrey Hepburn—lovely, elegant, and sophisticated—then Armagnac is more like Queen Latifah—beautiful, bold, and a bit wild. The volume of Armagnac produced is only about a tenth of that of Cognac, and yet it is one of only three brandy-making areas to have its own designation of origin classification, along with Cognac and the sherry-making region of Spain.

As with Cognac, Armagnac is also a place. It sits within the Gascony area in the department of Gers. This is in the southwest corner of France, directly below Bordeaux. This is the land of fois gras, black truffles, duck fat as a cooking medium, and the Three Musketeers. Armagnac blends seamlessly into this culinary landscape; its assertive flavors are a perfect marriage for the boldly flavored food. Armagnac is made from grapes grown in three distinct subregions, Ténarèze, Haut-Armagnac, and Bas-Armagnac. The brandies from Ténarèze tend to be light, floral brandies. Very little brandy is made these days from the Haut-Armagnac region, and those that are tend to be of lower quality despite the name (*haut* is "high" in French, but it refers to the elevation). The majority of the grapes, and the best quality brandies, come from the Bas-Armagnac, delicious examples that taste of prunes (for which the area is also noted) and plums, and they are more assertive and fragrant than their Cognac cousins.

By law, the grapes for Armagnac must be grown, and the spirit distilled, in the designated Armagnac region. Armagnac relies less on the Ugni Blanc grape than does Cognac. It makes up about 55 percent of the blend. The other grapes allowed for Armagnac are Folle Blanche, Colombard, Baco Blanc, and several others that are used in small proportions.

Armagnac is distilled only once in a unique version of the continuous still sometimes called an *alambic armagnacais*. Traditionally, most brandy producers in Armagnac didn't own their own stills, and so this type of continuous still, more compact than a pot still, was transported from farm to farm to distill each maker's wine. After distillation, the brandy is aged in oak barrels. In the past, black oak from nearby forests was the preferred medium. Scarcity of local wood, as well as economics, has prompted a change to other types of oak, typically similar to those used for Cognac. Armagnac is generally aged for at least a decade longer than cognac, but like cognac, the brandy starts out in new barrels and then later on is transferred to older, used barrels for the remainder of the aging period.

Armagnac uses a similar labeling code as Cognac, but unfortunately the codes mean slightly different ages. To add to the confusion, the Armagnacais use several different methods to indicate the age on the bottle:

- The first is to use the same series of letters as Cognac, that is, VS, VSOP, XO, and so on. In general, the average age of the youngest eau-de-vie in the blend is slightly older for Armagnac than Cognac by one or two years.

- In a second method, some prefer to simply state the age on the bottle, an indication of the average age of the brandies blended inside.

- The third method is to use a vintage, the year the grapes were harvested and the subsequent brandy was made. In this case, the contents of the bottle must all be from that vintage. Furthermore, vintage Armagnacs are usually labeled with the date of the bottling. The reason for this is that, like most spirits, once the brandy is put in a glass bottle, no further aging takes place, effectively freezing the spirit in time.

Despite the fact that so many people have thumped the Bible in the name of temperance, Jesus himself drank alcohol and approved of its moderate consumption (see the book of Matthew), and Saint Paul believed it to be a creation of God and a good thing. Even the early Christian church declared that alcohol was a gift from God to be used and enjoyed, and while abstention was okay, to despise alcohol was considered heresy.

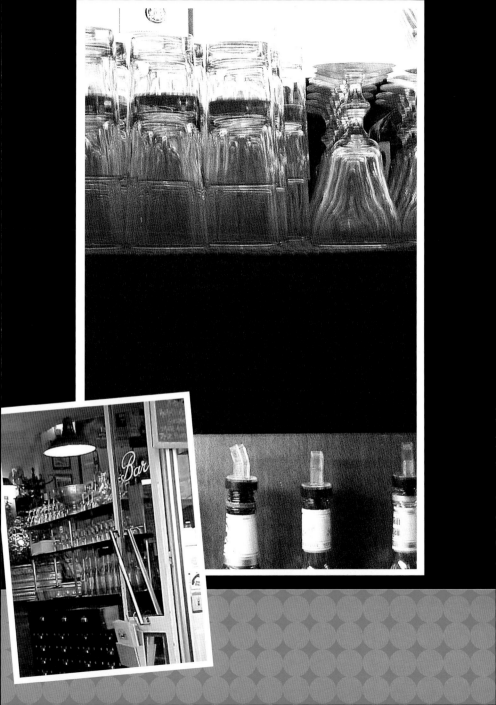

CALVADOS

For one country to have three different but equally fabulous examples of brandy—ones to which all others aspire—is, if nothing else, evidence that France is the greatest brandy region on earth. Calvados, the third brandy in the triad of great French spirits that includes Cognac and Armagnac, is made from the fermented juice of apples, for which the Normandy region is justly famous. Generally a fiery elixir that can also have great finesse and character, it can work well in cocktails. Calvados is distilled twice in a traditional pot still and is aged in oak barrels for a number of years. Although other apple brandies exist, such as our own applejack, Calvados is generally much more complex, often reaching the same qualitative heights as its grape-based counterparts.

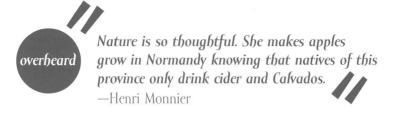

Nature is so thoughtful. She makes apples grow in Normandy knowing that natives of this province only drink cider and Calvados.
—Henri Monnier

The Calvados region is located within the historic region of Basse-Normandie on the northwest coast of France. One of the few regions of the country that has no significant wine production, Normandy instead has apples and a tradition of apple brandy so ensconced that one region has its own *appellation d'origine contrôlée* (AOC), a distinction normally reserved for wine regions. The Calvados area is bordered by the rivers Seine and Orne to the east and west, respectively. The coastal side, the Baie de Seine, is famous for the beaches upon which the Allied invasion landed during World War II. The area got its name from a Spanish ship, *El Calvador*, part of the armada that sank off the coast in the sixteenth century.

Norman farmers have made hard cider from their apples for centuries, and one area in particular, the Pays d'Auge, grows the best varieties and is the region that was awarded the prestigious AOC. Over thirty varieties of apples, out of more than one hundred grown, are used to make Calvados; many of them are small, like crab apples rather than eating apples. The method for making Calvados has remained virtually unchanged for hundreds of years:

1. The apples are basically smashed into a pulp called "pomace."

2. After resting for several hours, the juice is pressed out of the mash and left to ferment on its own naturally.

3. The fermented cider is double distilled in a traditional pot still, very similar to the ones used for Cognac.

4. The resulting eau-de-vie is then barrel aged for anywhere from two to thirty years.

5. Calvados is bottled at about 90 proof.

What are liqueurs?

Liqueurs are sweetened spirits flavored with any number of botanicals, such as roots, seeds, herbs, fruit, fruit peels, nuts, and so on. Many of the recipes date back centuries and were originally developed for medicinal purposes.

What's the difference between liqueurs and cordials?

They are the same. The term *cordial* is most often used in this country, probably because it doesn't sound so much like *liquor*.

How come some liqueurs have the same name but are made by different manufacturers?

Proprietary liqueurs, such as Cointreau, Kahlúa, and Grand Marnier, are specific blends that are unique to one producer. Generic liqueurs have a particular flavor that can be made by anyone such as crème de cacao, triple sec, or curaçao.

Is French vermouth always white and dry, and Italian vermouth always red and sweet?

The Italians were the first to make vermouth, and the style was sweet and aged in wood to attain color. The French followed with a dry version that is essentially clear. Over time, however, manufacturers from both countries have begun to make both varieties. Still, because of their origins, people sometimes refer to sweet vermouth as "Italian vermouth" and dry versions as "French vermouth." Our preference is a French version, Noilly Prat, for dry vermouth, and an Italian version, Martini & Rossi, for sweet, but there are others that are very good.

LIQUEURS, ANISE, BITTERS, AND VERMOUTH

The curious libations listed here include some of the oldest and the newest of all alcoholic drinks. They are all highly flavored, spirit-based concoctions, and the differences in classification are subtle. Most of them are much older than any of the main spirits in this book, while others are strictly twentieth-century inventions, with more being developed all the time. The oldest ones are closely related historically and were originally created for their curative effects, either for specific ailments or simply as health-inducing elixirs to soothe away the pains of life. Today, they're consumed mostly for pleasure, although some, particularly the bitters category, are still used as a digestive or to settle an upset tummy. Many people only consume liqueurs and their ilk as components of modern cocktails, while others prefer them straight or on the rocks. We've sorted them into four major categories, though, in truth, many could fit neatly into more than one group.

As we said, the differences are sometimes subtle, but, generally speaking, liqueurs are sweet by nature, whereas bitters are, well, bitter. Anise-flavored liqueurs, such as pastis, were developed as an alternative to the notoriously sinister absinthe (more about that later). Vermouth is actually wine based but is fortified with spirits and comes in both sweet and dry varieties. Whether these various spirits are used as modifying agents in cocktails or simply sipped neat after dinner, they have become indispensable for both drinking establishments and the home bar. A general understanding of how they're made, and from what, will be a boon to anyone who wishes to serve them or wants to create their own cocktails.

LIQUEURS

Unless you only want to drink spirits straight, liqueurs—and one or two in particular—are virtually indispensable at the bar. They add another dimension of flavor to many of our most cherished cocktails, providing a sweet counterpoint to the sourness of citrus and helping take the edge off the sharpness of the liquor. (A good bartender treads lightly here, for the base spirit should not be overwhelmed by the taste of liqueur, nor should the drink become cloyingly sweet.) Most liqueurs are also delightful on their own for sipping, either as an aperitif or after dinner.

Liqueurs are sweetened spirits with flavors and aromas derived from any number of plant sources, including herbs, nuts, seeds, roots, bark, fruit, fruit pits, and fruit peels, and they are typically classified according to the principal flavoring used. The quality of any liqueur depends on the selection and quality of the botanicals and the methods by which these flavorings are infused into the base spirit. Many liqueurs are based on medieval recipes intended originally as remedies or restoratives, elixirs that met with varying degrees of success. Some of the most famous proprietary brands, like Bénédictine and Cointreau, as well as several manufacturers, such as Bols and DeKuyper from Holland and Marie Brizard from France, have histories that go back centuries. Many of today's liqueurs are commercial versions of traditional recipes that are still made today in villages throughout Europe. Some of the liqueurs, such as Malibu, Alizé, and any number of alcoholic "coolers," were spawned by the increased popularity of these sweet and alluring concoctions among the young club-going crowd.

The oldest liqueurs, dating back to the Middle Ages, were developed by alchemists and apothecaries, who were mostly female before the formation of specialized trade guilds that excluded women. During centuries of war, plague, and the reigns of various ruthless tyrants, it was the monks in the local monasteries who kept the traditions alive. Those tippling friars would have had the time, resources, devotion, and necessary knowledge to experiment and refine these drinks, and the proceeds from selling the various liqueurs and bitters to the public would have helped to support their fraternal orders. The base spirits, or *eaux-de-vie*, would have been thought of as medicine, and the monks' instincts as alchemists would have

what's in a name?

The words *liqueur*, *liquor*, and *liquid* are all derived from the same Latin verb, *liquefacere*, meaning "to make liquid" or "to dissolve," an apt description of the whole process by which the flavors of various botanicals are extracted and left suspended in liquid, or in this case, spirits. *Cordial*, a term for liqueurs used mostly on this side of the Atlantic (although increasingly less so), stems from the Latin *cordialis*, or "pertaining to the heart," from *cor*, or "heart." Many of these blends were thought to aid the circulatory system, and hence the heart. Or perhaps they were simply used to mend a broken heart, as they so often are today.

naturally suggested the addition of beneficial herbs and such to further enhance the remedial qualities of the spirits. Additionally, the botanicals would have been better preserved in the spirit, a real boon in days before refrigeration.

Originally, liqueurs were sweetened with dates and honey, but once sugarcane production really took off in the Caribbean islands, sugar became the dominant sweetener. In fact, the two factors with the greatest influence on the formulation of modern liqueurs were cheap, abundant supplies of sugar from the Caribbean and the invention of the continuous still, which allowed for a steady supply of neutral grain spirits rather than the more costly and time consuming eau-de-vie.

All liqueurs begin with a spirit base into which flavors of some type of aromatic plant are infused. The most common forms of alcohol used are neutral grain spirits, but brandy, rum, and whiskey are also used, finished spirits that add their own distinctive character to the liqueur. Sugar is added, usually fine granulated sugar cooked into simple syrup, or, less commonly, honey. The sugar in a liqueur serves three purposes: it balances out the acidity of the distilled spirit; it tempers any bitterness; and it heightens the aroma. Liqueurs must have a minimum sugar content of 20 percent (or 200 grams of sugar per liter), but in practice they are usually much higher, typically around 35 to 40 percent (about 400 grams of sugar per liter). Liqueurs with the highest amount of sugar—40 percent or more—are known as "crèmes," as in crème de cacao or crème de menthe.

Schnapps constitutes another group of liqueur-like beverages. Some confusion arises here because it is also a term used in Scandinavia and Germany for aquavit (a clear distillate that is similar to vodka), though usually spelled schnaps. Schnapps as a liqueur is really akin to a flavored vodka, with the base spirit being made from almost anything including various types of grain and potatoes. They are sweetened and flavored with all kinds of spices and fruit, or in lesser versions with artificial flavors. American schnapps tend to be much sweeter than their European counterparts—more like a regular liqueur—and often contain glycerin. Most schnapps from Europe tend to rely solely on the fruit to give sweetness to the base spirit.

There are basically three ways to infuse flavors into a liqueur, and the type of flavoring to be used often dictates the method:

- Maceration: This is the most basic method and one that works best with delicate fruits that can't stand up to further distillation. The fruit is simply soaked in the spirit for several weeks or months until the flavors are thoroughly infused. In a similar method called "infusion" or "digestion," a heated spirit is poured over leaves or other plant sources, not unlike brewing tea.

- Percolation: If infusion is like steeping tea, percolation is like brewing coffee. The botanicals are suspended in a chamber over the spirit, a technique gleaned from the early perfume makers. The spirit is heated and pumped up though a central tube, from which it sprays out over the flavoring agent, dripping back down through to the bottom. This process continues until a sufficient amount of flavor has been extracted. Also, similar to brewing coffee, this method works best with things like cacao beans (chocolate), vanilla beans (typically used to enhance another flavor, such as chocolate), and, of course, coffee beans.

- Distillation: In this method, the aromatics are distilled in a pot still right with the spirit. The method is best with seeds like anise and caraway, citrus peels, some flowers, and some herbs, such as mint.

The use of artificial flavorings or chemically extracted essences is not common, but neither are they disallowed. However, the law stipulates that if these are used to make liqueurs the label must state either "imitation," "artificial," or, as they are required to say in France (whence many notable liqueurs hail), *fantaisie*. Along with the flavor and sweetness of liqueurs, the bold, bright, sometimes exotic colors are one of their most appealing attributes, especially to those who prefer to drink them straight. However, rarely does the color of a liqueur come from the actual flavoring element; it's usually added by using natural food colorings. Liqueurs are seldom aged for any length of time, if at all (although the base spirit may be aged, as in the case of whiskey), but they will often be set aside to rest in order for the flavors to properly "marry" with the spirit.

Actually, it only takes one drink to get me loaded. Trouble is, I can't remember if it's the thirteenth or fourteenth.
—George Burns

All liqueurs are blends, even those that display one prominent flavor, such as crème de banana or crème de cacao. Master blenders use dozens of flavorings to achieve subtle variations or to strengthen the flavor of the main ingredient. Liqueurs are usually sorted by the chief flavoring, such as nut liqueurs, fruit liqueurs, and so on. However they can also be divided into two general categories.

Generic liqueurs are those that have a particular flavor and can be made by virtually anyone. These include such types as all the crème liqueurs and triple sec, or curaçao. On the other hand, proprietary brands are specific blends unique to one producer, such as Cointreau, Grand Marnier, Kahlúa, and Baileys Irish Cream. Many of these proprietary blends have inspired imitations or have counterparts among the generic brands, as is the case with triple sec, but the generic versions are never quite the same as, and rarely as good as, the originals, made with closely guarded family recipes. Also, while the generics are more often based on neutral grain spirits, most proprietary brands use finished spirits, especially some type of brandy.

Think Americans drink a lot? Think again. At a mere 1.75 gallons of alcohol annually per person, as a nation we don't even make the top ten (we're number thirty-two on the list). The top ten tippling nations are (from one to ten) Portugal, Luxembourg, France, Hungary, Spain, Czech Republic, Denmark, Germany, Austria, and Switzerland.

What follows is a look at some of our favorite liqueurs, and those most commonly used at the bar today. These are all proprietary brands unless otherwise noted.

Amaretto This lovely amber-hued, almond-flavored liqueur is actually flavored with apricot pits, although sometimes crushed almonds are used to lend a more almondlike aroma. There are several brands of this generic liqueur made today, but the original, best known, and arguably the best is Disaronno, named for the village of Saronno in northern Italy near Lake Como. (It was originally named "di Saronno," which eventually became one word, no doubt to make it easier on English-speaking consumers.) Very good on its own—neat or on the rocks—amaretto is also a flavorful addition to such cocktails as a Godfather and an Amaretto Sour.

B & B   No, it's not a bed-and-breakfast. The initials simply stand for Bénédictine and brandy, which is exactly what it is. A twentieth-century invention, the mixture is approximately 60 percent Bénédictine and 40 percent Cognac, the latter cutting the sweetness considerably. The blend is redistilled for continuity. B & B is typically served neat or on the rocks.

Baileys Irish Cream   The first and best of the cream liqueurs, Baileys started a trend that has yet to let up. Bailey's is surely one of the greatest success stories of the spirits world, due in part to savvy marketing, but mostly because it is absolutely delicious and has garnered legions of fans. This alluring concoction starts with good Irish whiskey (of course) and fresh cream, to which are added natural flavorings, at the forefront of which are chocolate and vanilla. Baileys (or rather IDV, International Distillers and Vintners) developed the process whereby the cream and whiskey are completely homogenized and pasteurized, a process that may not be so good for cheese but that makes possible this delectable quaff. The result is a creamy, light brown sipping liqueur with subtle chocolate flavor and hints of vanilla. Although it's best served neat or in a cup of coffee, Baileys Irish Cream is found in several cocktails, including the Mudslide, the B-52, and the slightly lascivious Dirty Girl Scout.

Bénédictine D.O.M.   Allegedly the world's oldest liqueur, this herbal classic was first made around 1510 by the Bénédictine monks at their abbey in Fécamp, France. Legend has it (and who are we to argue with divine provenance?) that Dom Bernardo Vincelli received the recipe in a vision so that the monks could combat the plague, which always seemed to loom on the horizon in those days. The Cognac-based liqueur uses over two dozen herbs laced with orange peels and is aged for four years before being bottled. Today, Bénédictine D.O.M. is made by the Le Grand family and has been since about the time of our own Civil War; reportedly, Alexander Le Grand found the long-lost recipe, which had disappeared during the French

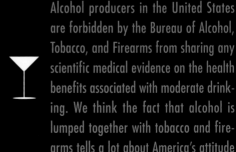

Alcohol producers in the United States are forbidden by the Bureau of Alcohol, Tobacco, and Firearms from sharing any scientific medical evidence on the health benefits associated with moderate drinking. We think the fact that alcohol is lumped together with tobacco and firearms tells a lot about America's attitude toward drinking.

Revolution when the abbey was destroyed. The monks gave the Le Grands permission to commercially produce their beloved liqueur with one stipulation, that the abbey's motto, *Dio Optimo Maximo* (D.O.M.), always appear on the label. For those who slept through Latin class, it means "To God, Most Good, Most Great." Bénédictine is usually served neat, but it does make an appearance in one cocktail, the Silent Monk, where it is combined with cream and Cointreau.

Chambord   Known as much for its distinctive spherical bottle—topped with a crown and wrapped in a metal band that bears the name—as it is for the viscous raspberry liqueur inside, this is one of the oldest liqueurs, dating back to the throne of Louis XIV. It's made with black raspberries and other fruits and uses honey as the sweetening agent. Its best use is perhaps as a topping for vanilla ice cream. Added to a glass of Champagne, it makes for a lovely variation on a Kir Royale (normally Champagne with a dash of crème de cassis).

Chartreuse   This liqueur has been made by Carthusian monks in the foothills of the French Alps for more than three hundred years. Reportedly made from 130 different botanicals, Chartreuse originally came in only the green variety, with a flavor redolent of mint and spices. The yellow version, with a lower alcohol content, was introduced in the early nineteenth century and uses a slightly different recipe that includes honey. To many people, the difference between the two flavors is very subtle, both tasting rather medicinal overall. Those who can discern a difference usually

describe the yellow one as mellower and sweeter. A small amount of each type is set aside for further aging each year. These VEP varieties (*Vieillissement Exceptionnellament Prolongé*, or "exceptionally long aging") are aged up to twelve years in oak. And, in a chicken-or-the-egg conundrum, the yellow variety of Chartreuse has such a distinctive color that the color was named for the liqueur, not the other way around. Although it's used in a few obscure cocktails like the Golden Fleece, Chartreuse is typically served straight, neat, or on the rocks.

Cointreau   This brandy-based orange liqueur is the best-known version of curaçao. Still made from a secret recipe by the Cointreau family, its origins go back to the nineteenth century, when the scion of the founder went off to the New World to seek his fortune. His fortune, as it turned out, was in orange peels, the bitter variety such as those from Curaçao (see separate entry). He sent them back to his family in France where his father experimented with the aromatic peels and finally hit upon the recipe for this distinctive liqueur that is still used today. Cointreau is a double-distilled liqueur that has the distinction of being dry, or at least has a perceived dryness since it does indeed have sugar in it. Much drier than any other liqueur at the time, it was referred to as *triple sec* or "three times as dry," a moniker that has become a generic term for the cheaper imitations that abound. Cointreau, easily the most used liqueur at the modern bar, is an integral part of such classic cocktails as the Margarita, Lemon Drop, Cosmopolitan, Sidecar, and countless others. It is also pleasant to drink straight, either neat or on the rocks, typically after dinner.

Curaçao   The generic name for a liqueur flavored with dried, bitter orange peels, the most famous of which come from the Caribbean island of Curaçao, hence the name. The Dutch were the first to manufacture this liqueur, but today there are many imitations, most of them made in the United States. The best and most famous proprietary brands are Cointreau and Grand Marnier, both from France (see separate entries), and one that we love for our house margaritas, Gran Torres Orange Liqueur, a brandy-based version from Spain.

Drambuie   Here is another venerable old liqueur swathed in legend, this time from the moors of Scotland. After his defeat at the hands of the British in 1745 during the ill-fated Scottish rebellion, Bonnie Prince Charlie (Prince Charles Edward Stuart, aka The Pretender) was on the lam. In gratitude for sheltering him from his would-be captors, the prince gave the recipe for *an dram buidheach*, "the drink that satisfies," to his host, a Captain MacKinnon. Supposedly, the family kept the recipe for their own use until just after the turn of the twentieth century, when they began to offer it commercially; the recipe is still a closely held family secret. The base of Drambuie, the anglicized version of the name, is Scotch whisky, which is combined with various herbs and spices and sweetened with honey. It is doubtless very similar to other Celtic concoctions made in the early era of whisky production in the British Isles, known generally as "heather wines." It's lovely as an after-dinner cordial, neat like Scotch, or combined with Scotch in a classic cocktail, the Rusty Nail.

Frangelico   The tall brown bottle in the shape of a robed friar (no doubt Fra Angelico) is a familiar sight in bars everywhere. It is flavored predominantly by hazelnuts and herbs and is supposedly based on a three-hundred-year-old elixir made by the hermit monk himself from nuts, berries, and wild herbs he gathered in the woods. In addition to being a very pleasant sipping liqueur, either neat or on the rocks, it can be added to coffee and has found its way into some amusingly named cocktails, such as the Friar Tuck.

Galliano   Thanks to the Harvey Wallbanger (vodka, orange juice, and Galliano), that iconic take on the classic Screwdriver from 1960s surfer bars, Galliano is here to stay. Named for the Italian hero of the Italian-Abyssinian War, Major Giuseppe Galliano, it's an herby, orangey, slightly anise-flavored, vanilla-laden liqueur. Rarely consumed on its own, it continues to be an ingredient in a few cocktails, such as the Golden Dream.

Godiva chocolate liqueur   There are several other proprietary brands of chocolate liqueur, some of them combining chocolate with other flavorings, such as mint, coffee, fruits, and nuts. There are also many generic versions, called "crème de cacao," any of which will work just fine in cocktails calling for chocolate flavoring. Our favorite, however, is Godiva, made by the venerable Belgian chocolate house. It has a deep, rich chocolaty flavor that makes for a very decadent Chocolate Martini.

Grand Marnier   Surely one of the greatest liqueurs ever has to be Grand Marnier, especially the two reserve blends they issued for their hundredth and hundred-and-fiftieth anniversaries, the Cuvée du Centenaire and Cuvée du Cent Cinquantenaire, respectively. Grand Marnier is a lovely, amber-colored liqueur based on Cognac and flavored with the peels of bitter oranges from the Caribbean, mainly Haiti. The original recipe dates back to 1827, when Jean-Baptiste Lapostolle first settled on the right combination of flavors. The aforementioned cuvées use only Fine Champagne Cognac, which adds depths of flavor and an extra toastiness to the mix. Grand Marnier is superior to other curaçao-type liqueurs as a cordial to be sipped straight, either neat or over ice. It also makes an exceptional ingredient in cocktails, especially the Margarita, where it stands up well to the añejo tequilas. Grand Marnier is also frequently called for in dessert recipes.

Kahlúa   When this coffee-flavored liqueur first hit the United States in the early 1960s, it took the country by storm, mostly as a component of cocktails, such as Kahlúa and Cream or the Black or White Russian (both based on vodka, which was also coming into vogue at the time). It has a neutral spirit base and is flavored with not only coffee beans but also vanilla and cacao beans. It is without a doubt still the country's favorite coffee liqueur, aided in part by its distinctive tall bottle with the big yellow label. Kahlúa is seldom consumed on its own but continues to be a fixture in bars everywhere.

Maraschino liqueur   Luxardo, our favorite brand of this generic liqueur, is really more of an eau-de-vie, with elements of grappa thrown in. Maraschino liqueur is made from marasca cherries grown in Italy and Dalmatia, a region of what used to be Yugoslavia. Both the pulp and the pits of the cherries, left over from making cherry wine (hence the reference to grappa), are distilled to a clear, relatively dry liqueur. It is used primarily in mixed drinks and no longer bears any relation to the industrially made maraschino cherry found in the bottom of a Manhattan.

Midori melon liqueur   The bright, neon green of this Japanese liqueur can be off-putting, but it's actually quite delicious and figures into all sorts of modern cocktails, including variations on the Martini. Made by Suntory, the huge distillery better known for their malt whiskies, this brand of melon liqueur has also spawned several domestic imitations, but if you're going to use melon liqueur, stick to Midori.

Sloe Gin   Not a gin at all, this generic liqueur surely evokes odious memories of clandestine teenage parties and first-time hangovers. Made with neutral spirits flavored (as any good crossword solver can tell you) with sloe berries from the blackthorn bush, sloe gin is mainly used as a mixer, or for spiking the punch at the prom.

Tia Maria   If you've ever wondered why it's so difficult to find real Jamaica Blue Mountain coffee, it's either because the Japanese have bought it all, or because it's the principal flavoring in this luscious liqueur. This is another brand with a lengthy heritage, supposedly dating back to the middle of the seventeenth century, when the British took over the island nation of Jamaica from the Spanish (hence the Spanish name, meaning "Aunt" Maria). Apparently, the family recipe was passed from generation to generation for nearly three hundred years before the family gave permission for it to be commercialized. Drier and lighter than Kahlúa, Tia Maria is called for in a number of cocktails, such as the Velvet Hammer, the Blue Mountain, and the Tidal Wave.

Tuaca Although it sounds as though it should hail from an ancient Aztec recipe, this liqueur with citrus, vanilla, and herb flavors is from Italy. Relatively new to the American market, it hasn't been around long enough to figure into many cocktail recipes, but it's probably only a matter of time.

Vanilla schnapps As a flavoring, vanilla is too often taken for granted, but its ability to enhance other flavors, particularly chocolate, makes vanilla the ubiquitous ingredient that it is. Cocktails are no exception, and a good vanilla schnapps is important to have in the bar for drinks like Chocolate Martinis and Mudslides. Our favorite brand of this generic liqueur is Dr. McGillycuddy's, a clear, sweet liqueur with a pure vanilla flavor that is a result of using both whole vanilla beans and extract.

ANISE LIQUEURS

The general category of anise liqueurs, the most famous of which are Pernod and Ricard, is unique in the world of spirits and liqueurs. What sets them apart is their tendency to be less sweet than most liqueurs, as well as their lineage—both are based on the notoriously hallucinogenic absinthe, which has been banned in most of the world since around 1915. Achieving almost cult status during the grand time of the Belle Epoque, absinthe provided inspiration and inebriation to many of the twentieth century's most intriguing artists and writers, such as Toulouse-Lautrec, Picasso, Baudelaire, and Vincent van Gogh, an avid consumer who allegedly drank bottles of the stuff during the days just prior to cutting off part of his ear and subsequently taking his own life. Many have speculated on absinthe's role in Van Gogh's unraveling, and it certainly didn't help the liqueur's reputation any. Was it the absinthe, or was Van Gogh slowly going mad on his own and the drink simply put him over the edge? The truth is probably somewhere in the middle.

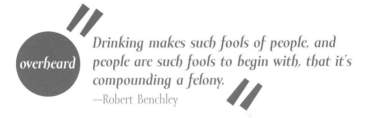

overheard

Drinking makes such fools of people, and people are such fools to begin with, that it's compounding a felony.
—Robert Benchley

Absinthe was referred to by fin de siècle Parisians as *la Fée Verte*, meaning "the Green Fairy," no doubt an allusion to the drink's alleged hallucinatory properties. French authorities were concerned that the unbridled consumption of absinthe would create mayhem, that people would go crazy from drinking it, and that there would be increased crime and rioting in the streets. It also presented some major competition to French winemakers, which may have had as much to do with its banishment as any concerns for health and public safety. Absinthe is distilled from a plant called "wormwood"; unfortunately, the wormwood also contributed a chemical known as "thujone," which may have been responsible for all the bad behavior. A few years ago, scientists at the University of California at Berkeley found that absinthe from that period contained alpha-thujone, a highly toxic form of the chemical that can poison the nervous system and create all kinds of havoc on one's frame of mind. Doubtless the alcohol level of absinthe—around 140 proof—helped cause a few lost weekends as well.

Absinthe was invented and manufactured by Pernod Fils, a company that was forced to close shop after absinthe was banned. Founder Henri-Louis reformatted the original recipe to exclude the wormwood, resulting in Pernod as we know it today, an anise-flavored liqueur that's much sweeter than absinthe and far less troublesome. Anise or aniseed comes from *Pimpinella anisum*, a plant native to the Levant that has been used to flavor various kinds of foods since classical times. Both the leaves and the seeds of the plant have pronounced licorice-like flavor (licorice is actually a different plant altogether), but it is principally the seeds, flavored by the essential oil anethole, that are used for liqueurs. Today, there are two major types of anise-flavored liqueurs.

Anisette Also known as "anis," this category includes Pernod, certainly the most famous of the group. They tend to be sweet, low-alcohol liqueurs with the unmistakable flavor of anise. Anisettes are defined by the fact that the spirits are distilled along with the botanical flavorings, which in the case of Pernod is only anise. Generic versions in this category often include various other flavorings, such as orange or other citrus fruits. This type of liqueur is common throughout the Mediterranean area. The Greeks, for example, have their ouzo (a drier aperitif not unlike grappa) and the Turks their raki. American brands (Arrow, Leroux, Hiram Walker) tend to be sweeter than their European counterparts, such as the Marie Brizard brand or Pernod.

Pastis This liqueur differs from anisette in that it achieves its anise flavor through maceration rather than distillation, and often licorice is used in addition to anise. The most famous brand of pastis is Ricard, although there are several other excellent brands that we like and use often in cocktails and by themselves. Names to look for are Granier Prado, the aforementioned Ricard, and Versinthe. A new, legal absinthe is available on the market now as well, made from southern wormwood—although related to the notorious wormwood, it apparently contains far less thujone. Absente, as the brand is called, is a mere 110 proof rather than absinthe's heady 140 proof.

Both anisette and pastis find themselves as ingredients in cocktails but are more often enjoyed the same way that absinthe once fueled the art crowd at the Moulin Rouge, typically consumed either neat or on the rocks, accompanied by a small pitcher of cold water. When the water is added, the drink suddenly becomes an opalescent yellowish white color. With absinthe, it was traditional to place a perforated spoon over the glass with a sugar cube on it. The water would be slowly dripped through the sugar, sweetening the absinthe. This step is usually omitted today, as anisettes and pastis are much sweeter than absinthe.

BITTERS

It's a fine line between bitters and liqueurs, with some spirits, like Campari, fitting easily into both categories. Bitters are based on old traditional medicinal remedies for settling upset stomachs, quelling fever associated with malaria and other tropical diseases, or serving simply as a digestive; many are still used solely for their remedial value. Like liqueurs, bitters are spirit based and flavored with all manner of roots, bark, and just about any other plant part. In addition to being used to enhance digestion, bitters are a common ingredient in cocktails and mixed drinks. Most of them are fairly high in alcohol, which, in addition to their strong flavor, is why they're used sparingly. They make possible the Manhattan, the Champagne Cocktail, and various other drinks, including a simple glass of seltzer water livened with a dash or two of bitters. The following are the most well-known varieties of bitters and the ones to consider having behind the bar.

Amer Picon   This French bitters contains, among other ingredients, gentian, cinchona bark, and bitter orange, and dates back to the 1830s. Typically enjoyed on the rocks with soda and an orange slice, this spirit also has its own cocktail, the aptly named Amer Picon Cocktail, made with fresh lime juice and grenadine.

Angostura bitters   This one literally began as a tonic to combat the tropical illnesses that beset Simón Bolívar's troops fighting for independence in South America. It was developed by Bolívar's surgeon general, Johann Siegert, in the early nineteenth century. The name comes from the former name of the Venezuelan port city now known as Ciudad Bolívar. At 90 proof, Angostura is quite strong, so it is used only drops at a time in such classic drinks as the Manhattan and the Champagne Cocktail. It's made from gentian and numerous other botanicals, the exact list of which is a closely guarded family secret.

Campari   Along with Angostura, Campari is the bitters best known to the world at large. Invented by Gaspare Campari in 1860, it is still served daily in its eponymous bar at the entrance to the Galleria in Milan, almost always as Campari and soda in specially designed glasses. In fact, Campari and soda is so popular and ubiquitous that the company actually bottles a premixed version that's sold around the world. The bright red bitter liqueur, flavored with dozens of herbs and fruits, has a sweetness that off-sets the bitterness. Unlike most bitters, Campari is preferred as a before-dinner drink, preparing the belly for what's to come. Next to its role as a pleasant aperitif, Campari is most famous as one of the principal ingredients in the Negroni and its less-alcoholic version, the Americano.

Cynar In this curious Italian bitter liqueur, the dominant flavor is that of artichokes, or artichoke leaves to be exact. Like Campari, Cynar is typically consumed before dinner as an aperitif, and if there's a cocktail out there calling for Cynar, it's news to us.

The Journal of Clinical Epidemiology reported that the U.S. government actually discourages public knowledge of the health benefits of moderate drinking. Here's an example: A study funded by the National Institutes of Health (NIH) found moderate drinkers to be less likely to suffer heart disease. The NIH wouldn't allow the Harvard researcher who conducted the study to publish his results because they considered them "socially undesirable."

Fernet Branca   Intensely bitter and medicinal tasting, Fernet Branca is definitely an acquired taste, and one that most of us never acquire. Invented in Milan in 1845 by Maria Scala, who later married into the Branca family, it was intended as an elixir to alleviate stomach ailments or to settle the tummy after a meal. *Fernet* refers to a hot poker, a tool used to stir the mash in the early days. The forty herbs and spices used to make Fernet Branca are a closely guarded family secret, as is the case for so many liqueurs. It is the number one digestive in Europe.

Peychaud's   It was dubbed a panacea when New Orleans apothecary Antoine Peychaud introduced his eponymous bitters in 1793. Besides being the inventor and namesake of these now-famous bitters, Monsieur Peychaud figures into two legends that place him securely in the history of spirits and cocktails. First, he's said to have invented what was to become the Sazerac, a cocktail originally calling for the Sazerac brand of French brandy (these days it's mostly made with whiskey but still calls specifically for Peychaud's bitters). Second, it's said that he served his mixed drinks in little eggcups, known in French as *coquetiers*. This is thought by many to have inspired the term cocktail, though there are several other theories. We remain dubious.

Punt e Mes   Is it a bitters or a vermouth? Technically, and diplomatically, Punt e Mes is a bitter vermouth, but we include it here because it is most often used as a bitters. It's made by the Carpano company in the Piedmont region of Italy, and has been since the late eighteenth century. The name relates to the Turin Stock Exchange, where a "point and a half," or *punt e mes*, was a common term. The story goes that a member of the exchange absentmindedly used the term to order his vermouth at the local café, and that this spirit has been known as such ever since. Punt e Mes is usually served over ice or straight up and very cold (we keep ours in the refrigerator). It can also replace vermouth, especially sweet vermouth, in cocktails like the Negroni.

VERMOUTH

Within the general category of wine there are four classifications: still, sparkling, fortified (this includes sherry, port, and Madeira), and aromatized. The most well-known of the latter is vermouth, one of the oldest spirits ever produced. Vermouth is also slightly fortified with grape spirits, which help preserve it, but it is vermouth's layers of flavorings for which it is known and used. The idea of adding various botanical flavorings to wine is no doubt as old as wine itself, and was certainly practiced by both the early Greeks and the Romans. In those days, however, it was done more for its remedial value, or to mask inferior-tasting wine, than for the virtues of the flavorings themselves. Today, vermouth—both sweet and dry—is a popular aperitif; a component of many great cocktails, including the Manhattan and the Negroni; and, most famously, one part of the triad upon which the Martini stands.

The name *vermouth* probably stems from either the German *wermut* or the Old English *wermod*, both meaning "wormwood" (*Artemisia absinthium*), the allegedly hallucinogenic shrub or bitter herb that is the main ingredient for absinthe, and one of the original ingredients of vermouth. Wines infused with wormwood have been used as medicinal elixirs for centuries, up to and including the Renaissance. It is rarely used for vermouth anymore, although some makers still include it in their proprietary recipes, which are closely guarded secrets. Several dozen aromatics are used to make vermouth, with some manufacturers claiming to use more than one hundred different plant sources that can include allspice, angelica, angostura, anise, bitter almond, bitter orange, blessed thistle, celery, chamomile, cinchona, cinnamon, clove, coca, coriander, elderflower, fennel, forget-

> *The wine urges me on, the bewitching wine, which sets even a wise man to singing and to laughing gently and rouses him up to dance and brings forth words which were better unspoken.*
> —Homer, *The Odyssey*

overheard

me-not, gentian, ginger, hops, mace, marjoram, myrtle, nutmeg, peach, rhubarb, rosemary, saffron, sage, sandalwood, savory, thyme, vanilla, and woodruff, to name just a few.

Vermouth as we know it today was first made in the Piedmont region of Italy in the late seventeenth century. Ironically, the first brand-name vermouth was Carpano's Punt e Mes, a bitter variety that belies Italy's reputation for sweet (*rosso*) styles of vermouth. Virtually all of the Italian vermouths made in the nineteenth century would be sweeter, one of which, Martini & Rossi, is arguably the most famous brand worldwide. French producers in and around Marseille began making a dry version from the local white wines around 1800, perhaps the most famous of which is Noilly Prat, widely considered to be one of the finest varieties available. These basic styles of production continued into the twentieth century, so much so that people still refer to sweet, or red, vermouth as Italian, and the drier, white vermouth as French. While this is still generally true, both sweet and dry versions are made in both Italy and France.

the
REALM
of the
MIXED-UP
SPIRITS

COCKTAIL TERMS

Neat
Any spirit or liqueur served on its own at room temperature (or cold if the bottle is taken from the refrigerator) with no ice.

Straight up, or simply up
This is a drink that is shaken or stirred, then strained into a cocktail glass. In other words, it's cold but served without ice. It can be a mix of spirits or one single spirit. Many cocktails, such as a Margarita, can be served straight up or on the rocks, as one prefers.

On the rocks
A spirit or cocktail served over ice ("rocks"), usually in an old-fashioned glass.

Highball
A somewhat ambiguous term, and one that is not used as much these days, although like the Old-Fashioned it has its own glass. Basically, a highball consists of one spirit and a mixer, with little or no garnish. It's a very quick drink to make, as implied by the original meaning of the name. In old railroad terminology, a highball—a ball placed high atop a pole—was the signal for the engineer to increase speed. Club soda was undoubtedly the original mixer in highballs, but today the choices are varied, from tonic to ginger ale, cola, and various other flavored sodas. Even a Screwdriver (vodka and orange juice) is essentially a highball, though the term classically refers to spirits mixed with some sort of soda or water. Classic examples of a highball include Scotch and soda, bourbon and water, 7 & 7 (Seagram's 7 and 7 Up), and rum and Coke (which becomes a Cuba Libre when lime is added).

Dirty
A Martini term meaning some of the brine from the cocktail olives is added to the drink.

COCKTAILS
Theory and Practice

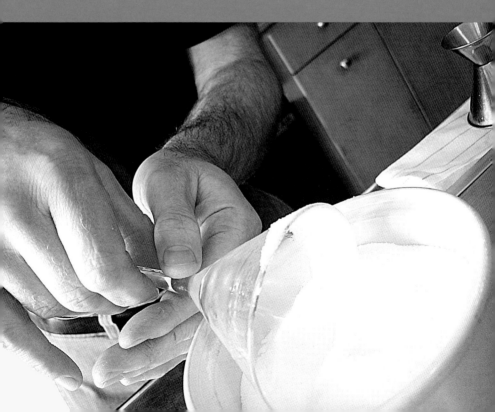

THEORY

Like jazz, banjos, tap dancing, and Westerns, cocktails are a uniquely American invention, albeit made and enhanced by spirits and liqueurs from all over the world. We by no means hold a monopoly on them, however, and today they are served in small bars, big hotels, and cafés and restaurants, and even on beaches throughout the world. Cocktails are arguably the most popular way of imbibing spirits, especially in the United States, even though the level of skill with which they're made varies considerably from bartender to bartender, and from bar to bar. Cocktails have become an indelible part of modern adult life—from Martinis and simple highballs to elaborate drinks involving several ingredients and fancy garnishes. Cocktails are very democratic too—accessible to anyone willing to spend a little time to learn how to make them correctly.

Although versions of mixed drinks were known and enjoyed prior to the twentieth century, cocktails as we know them today really came into full bloom during the decade of the 1920s, a time we now nostalgically refer to as the "jazz age." It was a time of unbridled optimism, great music, exciting nightclubs, and, not coincidentally, a time when ice was in ready supply more than ever before. Ironically, it was also a time when the entire country—officially at least—was dry, as mandated by the Volstead Act of January 17, 1920, a constitutional amendment that prohibited the manufacture, sale, and consumption of alcoholic beverages. It remains an example of how a small group of narrow-minded, self-righteous wet blankets were able to force their own twisted set of morals on the whole country, and how spineless, sycophantic politicians let it happen. (Do we sound bitter?) Lasting a little over a decade, Prohibition was repealed December 5, 1933, ending just in time, because by then the country was deep into the Great Depression and one can only assume that everyone was badly in need of a drink.

The resurgence in popularity of the cocktail in recent years has been driven at least in part by our appetite for bolder flavors in both our food and our beverages. This has allowed bars and bartenders to expand their offerings, in terms of both cocktail recipes and selection of spirits. One result of this newfound enthusiasm for spirits and cocktails has been a trend toward calling for one's preferred brand of spirits in a cocktail (typically premium brands), as in a Maker's Mark Manhattan or a Ketel One Martini. The reason for this is surely more than simply looking knowledgeable in front of one's date. In the case of a straightforward drink like a Martini, it may be that through trial and error the drinker has come to prefer one brand over another. In the case of more complex drinks, where the particular spirit is not so readily identifiable, it may simply be to ensure getting a quality spirit. In other words, such customers may not be able to pick out their brand of vodka in a blind tasting, but they at least know they're getting a better drink than if they simply order a Screwdriver or a Cosmopolitan. Fortunately, the trend has been for bar owners to steer away from rotgut brands and upgrade their house selections to be more in line with the overall quality of the establishment. In fact, even though at one time cocktails were used to mask cheap, indifferently made alcohol, today they are more often used to enhance well-made alcohol. That's good news for everyone, except perhaps for companies who make cheap liquor.

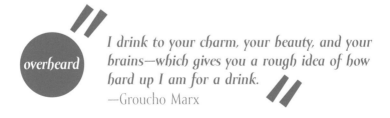

I drink to your charm, your beauty, and your brains—which gives you a rough idea of how hard up I am for a drink.
—Groucho Marx

The earliest known mention of the term *cocktail* in relation to a mixed drink was in 1806, not an era we normally equate with swizzle sticks and cocktail parties, but where exactly the term came from has been a matter of research and speculation ever since. There are countless theories in countless cocktail books, and now, two hundred years later, we may have to accept that the answer is forever shrouded in the mists of history. It doesn't really matter, except as fodder for great arguments at the bar, but there are some truly inspired stories as to the word's genesis and we relate a few of them here:

- There are several tales that involve a reference to a "cock's tail" around the time of the American Revolution, and it usually hangs on some publican's favorite fighting rooster, or cock. One even has it that a pub owner offered his daughter's hand in marriage to anyone who returned to him his lost bird. Of course, the suitor whom she really loves brings back the bird, having taken it himself for just that reason. All the stories end with the lovely barmaid concocting a mixed drink with which everyone offers a rousing toast to the cock's tail. Similar tales have the barmaid mixing drinks with a cock's tail for passing soldiers, which seems awfully unsanitary; we're glad that tradition has lapsed into history.

- Others have asserted that *cocktail* is a racing term. In one version, unscrupulous traders allegedly fed spirits to their horses to cock their tails and make them seem perkier than perhaps they really were. Another theory recalls the term *cock-tailed*, used for non-Thoroughbred horses because their tails were cropped to distinguish them as mixed breeds.

- The allure of cockfighting has always eluded us, but the sport has produced at least one theory relating to cocktails: cock's ale was apparently a common mixed drink to serve at these bloody events.

- One of the most specific theories involves Antoine Peychaud, the creator of Peychaud's Bitters and perhaps the inventor of the Sazerac cocktail, who used to offer various brandy-based elixirs out of his apothecary shop in New Orleans, served in eggcups known in French as *coquetiers*.

PRACTICE

Making cocktails is easy and fun, and is a great way to enliven any kind of gathering. In addition to the spirits, liqueurs, and mixers needed to make mixed drinks, cocktails require only a few simple tools and the willingness to learn some basic techniques. One overriding principle should be addressed from the outset, whether you're making highballs or Hurricanes, and it is this: the better the ingredients you put into a drink, the better that drink will be. This tenet is not exclusive to making cocktails, holding true in almost any creative endeavor, from cooking to building skyscrapers. Use the best ingredients you have available. This does not necessarily mean you must always use the most expensive ingredients; rather, use the best ingredient for the particular application. For example, the finest single-malt Scotch is probably wasted in a cocktail that combines it with sweet liqueurs or vermouth. Likewise, if you're making a Chocolate Martini, you'll want to use a very high-quality chocolate liqueur for the best results, but you can be frugal when it comes to the vodka (please note that frugal doesn't mean cheap or bad liquor). As a general rule, use good quality spirits, liqueurs, and other mixers and you'll never go wrong.

Just what are the best quality spirits? We've made a point throughout this book to mention some of the better brands for sale across the country. In some cases, we've stated our preference for certain brands over others, either in a particular drink or in general, based on their flavor, method of production, and overall characteristics. If you're truly interested in increasing your knowledge of spirits but haven't been blessed with the Rockefeller fortune, there is a practical way to go about it. One of the great aspects of a good bar is that you can sample different brands and different styles of spirits without investing in whole bottles. If you like Martinis, for example, try ordering yours with a different brand of gin or vodka each time until you light on the one you like best. Maybe you'll be torn and have two or even three favorites. Don't worry. There's nothing in the rule book of life that says you can't have more than one favorite brand of booze.

While spirits play the starring role in any cocktail, it's important that the other ingredients you use also be of high quality. Stale juice, flat soda water, or indifferently made mixers will undermine all your efforts to obtain good quality spirits. With that in mind, here are a few thoughts on ingredients other than spirits:

- Whenever we call for the juice of lemons, limes, oranges, or grapefruit, we mean freshly squeezed. Lemons and limes are simple to squeeze to order with a handheld juicer (see Essential and Not-So-Essential Bar Tools), and just as fast as pouring out of a can. If you know you'll need a large quantity, make a batch right before the party begins. The same goes for oranges and grapefruit; juice them as close to the time you will want to use them as possible.

- For other juices like cranberry or pineapple, where it isn't practical to juice to order, be sure they're freshly opened. If you have leftovers from your last party, discard them and start with fresh juice.

- Use superfine sugar at the bar unless otherwise specified. It dissolves more quickly and completely than regular granulated sugar.

- Although in most cases garnishes are optional, we do think they serve a purpose. A good garnish should complement the drink aesthetically and add flavor, whether served in the drink or offered at the discretion of the consumer, as with a lime wedge on the rim of the glass.

Ever wonder why your ice cubes float? Well, we'll tell you anyway. Water expands by 9 percent when it freezes, becoming in the process lighter than water, and therefore it floats.

Ice is the cheapest ingredient in your bar, so don't skimp. Always buy more than you think you'll need. With few exceptions, liquor should be poured over ice, not the other way around. If you're shaking a drink but still serving it on the rocks, strain the drink over fresh ice in the glass. Never reuse ice in a shaker. When making a new drink, use fresh ice.

Simple syrups, or sugar syrups, are handy to have and are a good way to sweeten cocktails without sugar clouding the drink. They are easy to make, and they keep indefinitely in a covered container. Although they can be substituted for sugar in most recipes, be aware that when muddling is called for, sugar works better as it provides friction.

To make simple syrup, combine 1 cup of water and 1 cup of sugar in a saucepan over high heat. Cook, stirring constantly, until the sugar dissolves and the mixture reaches a full boil. Remove from the heat and chill. For mint syrup, add a half bunch of mint just as the syrup comes off the heat. Allow to steep for 15 minutes, then strain and chill. For lemon syrup, add a cup of lemon juice as the syrup comes off the heat, then chill. For ginger syrup, add a cup of peeled and coarsely chopped fresh ginger to the sugar and water. Follow instructions for making syrup. Allow to steep for 15 minutes after the syrup comes off the heat, then chill.

When a recipe calls for whipped cream, avoid using canned versions. They tend to be overly sweet and they never seem to have the same flavor and texture of the real thing. We like making ours with a cold bowl and a balloon whisk, but an electric mixer will work just as well except you'll miss out on the exercise.

GLASSWARE 101

The next solid principle to making good cocktails is to have the right glassware. While it's true that one could enjoy a cocktail out of a jelly jar if that drink is well made, part of the pleasure of drinking, as in so many things, is aesthetic. If you're going to make cocktails at home, and especially if you'll be serving them to friends, invest in the proper glassware. You don't, however, need to have as broad a selection as a bar might have, but only the basics for what you'll be serving. We've broken down the basics into three tiers. How many you choose should be dictated by your needs and your pocketbook. You'll also need an array of good wine and beer glasses.

PRIMARY BAR GLASSWARE

Martini glasses   These are often simply called "cocktail glasses," but whatever you call them, there is nothing more alluring sitting on the bar than a well-made cocktail served in a chilled martini glass. (There may be a more alluring sight sitting *at* the bar, but that's another story.) Use these for any cocktail served straight up. Avoid huge martini glasses, as the drink will generally get warm before you finish it. A good size is about 5 or 6 ounces. Keep martini glasses in the refrigerator or freezer so they're chilled when you need them.

Old-fashioned glasses   Although they bear the name of a famous cocktail, you can make all kinds of drinks in an old-fashioned glass, from simple Screwdrivers to Margaritas and more. This is also the best glass for serving straight spirits on the rocks.

Highball and/or collins glasses   The kind of tall glass we prefer is really a collins glass, but the nomenclature is cloudy here. (A Collins is a type of sour, made with virtually any spirit mixed with sugar, lemon, and club soda. See Tom Collins.) We feel the collins shape—tall and lean—is more versatile and better looking. Typically, a highball glass is a taller version of an old-fashioned glass. In a perfect world, you would have both highball and collins glasses. Throughout the recipes we have indicated one glass or the other, but the two can be substituted for one another.

SECONDARY BAR GLASSWARE

Brandy snifters   Banish those images of stuffy old men sitting around in their men-only clubs sipping brandy out of bulbous glasses the size of a small terrarium. At one time it was thought that large snifters better allowed the swirling vapors to release more of the bouquet. Modern oenologists have concluded, however, that in a glass that large, the vapors dissipate too quickly and the alcohol, when sniffed, is too intense. To present your finest brandies or single-malts at their best, select smaller, tulip-shaped snifters of about 4 or 5 ounces.

Champagne flutes   Besides being the perfect vessel from which to sip Champagne, Prosecco, Cava, or other sparkling wines, flutes are used for several cocktails, including a classic Champagne Cocktail and a Kir Royale (Champagne with a dash of crème de cassis). They can be a fun and festive way to serve other drinks as well.

Sherry glasses   Known in Spanish as *copitas*, these are the de facto glass for drinking any type of sherry. Additionally, they are perfect for liqueurs, port, or dessert wines, or for tasting wines and spirits.

Shot glasses   These can be the classic, Hollywood, knock-one-back-at-the-bar glasses, slightly splayed with faceted sides, or more elegant straight-sided glasses that are smaller versions of an old-fashioned glass. They are the perfect glass for serving spirits neat.

TERTIARY BAR GLASSWARE

Cordial glasses   Great for all sorts of eaux-de-vie—liqueurs as well as grappa and marc—the kind we like looks like a very small brandy snifter set on a tall stem, but there are dozens of designs available. Cordial glasses should be very elegant and help focus the bouquet of the spirit.

Heat-tempered glass mugs   Necessary for Hot Toddies, Irish Coffee, and other hot drinks. A 6- to 8-ounce size is usually sufficient.

ESSENTIAL AND
NOT-SO-ESSENTIAL BAR TOOLS

Whether you're making drinks at home for friends or opening your own bar, having the proper tools will make your job so much easier, and your drinks will look better too. Because of the resurgence in the popularity of cocktails, you will no doubt see all kinds of bar sets, typically very shiny and expensive, intended for the person who has everything. Some of these are well made and beautiful, but our experience has been that most of them are rather useless, designed by people who have never tended bar. You don't need to invest a fortune in tools to make great drinks. Besides, the drinks and the company in which one is drinking should be the focus, not your bar tools. Therefore, we recommend you go to either a serious kitchenware shop or a restaurant supply store to buy the necessary tools. Most of the items on this list are relatively inexpensive, but make sure to buy good-quality tools. Avoid plastic and other gimmicky paraphernalia unless no other options are available. As to the tools you will most need, one could easily make many good cocktails with nothing more than a shaker (Boston shaker), a strainer, a measuring device (especially for the beginner), and something to hold ice. If you want to entertain, however, and make a wide selection of cocktails, nothing on this list is really extraneous except where noted, and you could still be outfitted for probably less than $100.

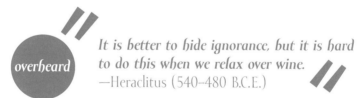

overheard

It is better to hide ignorance, but it is hard to do this when we relax over wine.
—Heraclitus (540–480 B.C.E.)

Bar spoon   Long stemmed with a bowl about the size of a teaspoon, a bar spoon is handy for everything from stirring your Manhattans to fishing a piece of cork out of a wine glass. The stem is usually twisted so that when rotated between the hands it goes up and down, but most bartenders usually just stir with it in a normal fashion.

Bar Towels   To really be set up for action, you'll need two types of bar towels: A terrycloth version is useful for cleaning up and wiping down the bar; they're very absorbent and once you have them you'll think of all kinds of uses. The other is a glass towel for polishing or drying glassware; they're smoother and lint free.

Blender   Frankly, we don't like electrical appliances around the bar. They take up valuable space, are tedious to clean, and most of what you can do—cocktail-wise—you can do in a good shaker. If you really want a blender, invest in a professional model, such as those made by Waring.

Boston shaker   Leave your antique collection of art deco cocktail shakers on the shelf for decoration. The only shaker worth using is the Boston shaker. It comes in two parts: a pint mixing glass and a slightly bigger stainless steel shaker top. They are much easier to use and clean than home-style cocktail shakers (see A Few Elementary Techniques), and the mixing glass portion can be used by itself when stirring drinks. The glass allows you to see what you're doing, which is useful if you're measuring by eye. The top then fits over the glass and you shake the drink. If it gets tight, which it probably will if you're shaking firmly, simply tap the edge of the metal cup on the edge of the counter and it loosens right away. A Hawthorne strainer (see Strainer) fits into either the glass or metal part. The metal cup is easier to pour from if you're aiming for a small opening or making two drinks at a time.

Bottle openers   Do we have to explain this one? Many beers and mixers still require an opener, and some twist-off caps can be very difficult, especially if one is arthritic. If you have a good corkscrew, it probably has a bottle opener on it.

Bottle stoppers   There are various designs of bottle stoppers, which are handy for keeping sodas bubbly without having to unscrew the cap each time. You can even save wine corks and pare them to fit any size bottle you have. A champagne stopper is very useful since you can't replace a champagne cork once it's out.

Corkscrew   If you drink wine, you probably already have a corkscrew and have opinions about them as well. We only recommend two styles of corkscrews. One is known as a "waiter's corkscrew." Once you learn how to use one, you'll never go back to anything else. They are compact and fit in your pocket, usually have a blade attachment for cutting foil, and are less likely to damage a cork. If you are intimidated by them or simply can't get the hang of it, the other type is called a "Screwpull." They are foolproof and efficient. They fit over the top of the bottle and all you have to do is keep turning the perpendicular handle until it draws the cork out. A corkscrew is essential even if you're not serving wine since many liqueurs and eaux-de-vie require one.

Cutting board   Duh. Unless you want to carve up that genuine tiki bar you just bought.

Grater   A small grater is useful for fresh nutmeg or citrus zest.

Ice container   It's nice to have an ice bucket for chilling wine, but for making cocktails you'll want something you can get a scoop into. In a professional bar, ice is kept in a large, stationary metal bin with a drain in the bottom, both to aid in cleaning at the end of the night and to keep the ice dry. Otherwise that ice will melt all night and you'll be scooping ice water into your drinks. Good alternatives include a cooler that can be kept behind the bar or even a clean stainless steel sink. In a pinch, simply place a large bag of ice in the sink and roll the top down.

Ice crusher   A small hand-cranked ice crusher is affordable and efficient enough for most uses, such as making Caipirinhas, Mojitos, and Mint Juleps, and much less annoying than an electric model. This is not absolutely essential since regular ice can be used in any drink that calls for crushed ice, although die-hard Kentucky Derby fans will probably disagree.

Ice scoop   Scoops are the fastest, most efficient way to fill your mixing glass without using your bare hands. The scoop should be big enough to fill a pint glass in one scoop.

Ice tongs   These are really more appropriate for Noel Coward plays than for serious bartending. However, if all you'll be doing is dropping a couple of ice cubes into your twenty-five-year-old Scotch, by all means grab the tongs.

Jigger   These come in many configurations, but the most common and useful is a stainless steel, hourglass-shaped measuring cup wherein one end is a "jigger," or 1 ½ ounces, and the other is a "pony," or 1 ounce. They are much faster than shot glass–style measuring devices, and you don't have to read the calibration on the side.

Juice dispensers   Here is one instance when plastic is better. A juice dispenser is a plastic bottle with a long neck and a speed pourer on top for pouring all sorts of juices and simple syrup. They're very handy if you're making drinks for a crowd and are indispensable for a professional bar. You can also use whatever pitchers you already have. Always start any cocktail session with fresh juice.

Juicers for lemons and limes   Our favorite handheld juicer hails from Mexico but is easy to find in any good kitchenware shop. We prefer chrome, but they also come in cast aluminum and enameled steel. This simple device flips open to hold one half of the fruit, and when you squeeze it, the fruit is inverted and completely juiced. They are quick, portable, easy to clean, and very efficient.

Juicers for larger fruit   There is no substitute for freshly squeezed citrus juices at the bar. There are several different types of juicers available, both electric and hand powered. Pick one that suits your needs, your space, your skills, and your pocketbook, and always serve fresh juice.

Knife   No great mystery here—you'll need a good paring knife, preferably serrated, for cutting up all kinds of fresh fruit for juice and garnishes.

Muddler   This wooden pestle looks like a miniature baseball bat and is used for crushing mint in a Mojito, fruit in an Old-Fashioned, and so on. You can do the same thing with the back of your bar spoon, but a muddler works better and they are inexpensive.

Speed pourers   Made to fit into just about any bottle of spirits or liqueur, speed pourers are essential for pouring quickly and accurately. The kind we like has a square spout with a grid over the end to help keep critters out of the bottle. It's a good idea to soak them in hot water between uses, especially with liqueurs where the sugar can build up and make them difficult to pour through.

Strainer   A strainer is necessary only if you're using a Boston shaker. There are basically two kinds: One is like a large, round, perforated spoon that must be held in place while pouring; they can be a little awkward and require practice. The kind most bartenders prefer is called a "Hawthorn strainer." It's flat with a coiled wire that runs around the edge. This coil fits snugly into the top of either the mixing glass or the steel shaker and holds the ice back. They are very easy to use and inexpensive, so buy two.

Straws and stirrers   Larger straws are good for tall drinks, sodas, and kids' drinks. Short, thin straws add an elegant touch to drinks served in old-fashioned glasses, and are especially useful for drinks that are intended to be stirred by the drinker.

Stripper   No, we're not referring to Gypsy Rose Lee. The stripper is a tool often found in tandem with a zester. While a zester has several tiny blades to take fine shreds of peel off citrus fruits, the stripper has a single channel to quickly and evenly pare off a thin strip of citrus peel for garnish. If the motion is executed directly over the drink, it will spritz a bit of essential oil over the surface of the drink and do more to flavor a cocktail than a dried out, precut lemon twist ever could.

Toothpicks or cocktail picks   So you don't have to fish that olive out of your Martini with your fingers.

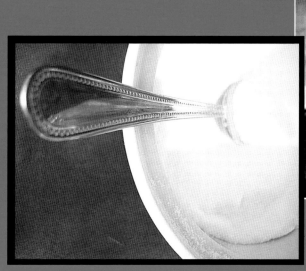

A FEW ELEMENTARY TECHNIQUES

Making good cocktails isn't brain surgery, but there are a few techniques that are necessary to know, all of which are simple and easy to master:

- Salting a rim: Have plenty of kosher salt in a saucer. Rub a freshly cut lime or lemon around the edge of the glass. Invert the glass and dip the the outer edge in the salt.

- Sugaring a rim: Have plenty of superfine sugar in a saucer. The sugar will adhere to a cold glass right from the freezer. Simply invert the glass and roll the outer edge around in the sugar. If the glass is warm, rub the outer edge with freshly cut lime or lemon, depending on the citrus used in the drink.

- Shaking a cocktail in a Boston shaker: Fill the mixing glass with ice cubes. For one drink, the combined ingredients should fill half the glass; two cocktails will fill the glass almost to the top. Place the metal shaker on top securely and shake well. Remove the metal top. If it's stuck, hold it so the metal cup is on top and lightly tap the rim on the edge of the counter; it will pop loose. Place a strainer over the mixing glass and pour the drink into the desired glass, straining out the used ice. It's easier to pour from the metal shaker, especially if mixing two drinks at once. Note that when making a Collins or any other shaken drink served over ice, you should always strain the drink over fresh ice in the glass.

- Layering: This technique is used to create layered liqueur drinks, or pousse-cafés, such as the B-52. Start by pouring in the heaviest ingredient (the recipe should list the liqueurs in order of weight). Then, pouring slowly over the back of a spoon, pour in the next-lightest ingredient. Repeat with as many ingredients as are called for.

- Muddling: Place the ingredients to be muddled in the bottom of the glass they will be served in, or in some cases, the mixing glass. Typical ingredients that call for muddling are mint leaves, pieces of fruit, and sugar. Simply use the muddler to lightly crush the ingredients in order to release either their juice or their aroma as in the case of mint leaves. When the ingredients are sufficiently crushed, proceed with the recipe.

ixing cocktails that will enhance your efforts: In many of the recipes, we've named a specific
lcohol, either because it's a proprietary blend, such as Campari or Kahlúa, or because of our per
erence. In the case of the latter, feel free to substitute your favorite brand, which may just be the b
happen to have on hand.

arding the use of Cointreau, Grand Marnier, and other orange-based liqueurs, easily the most
e of liqueur at the bar, we are well aware of the inflated price of some of these brands, espe
ntreau. Therefore, in some cases, such as for the Margarita, we simply call for an orange-based lique
ain cases, where a particular proprietary brand is traditional, we call for it by name. We do recom
esting in good-quality orange liqueurs such as Cointreau, Grand Marnier, or Gran Torres O
ueur. As with any other ingredient, the better the quality, the better the drink.
ile we think the proportions in the recipes here are correct, don't be afraid to improvise. Perhap

es Bond's famous admonition that he preferred his Martinis shaken, not stirred has caused constern
I debate ever since. W. Somerset Maugham advised to stir "so that the molecules lie sensuously on t
another." Others warn that too rough a treatment will "bruise" the gin. Hmm. We think you can t
apple, bruise your shin, and even bruise your ego, but we have never been convinced that you can t
Although you can make a good Martini by either method, the principal objective should be to
the drink is very cold and well mixed. Therefore, we go with Bond on this one and recom
king your Martinis, as this is the best and easiest way to ensure your Martini will be the proper tem

COCKTAIL RECIPES

While most fine spirits can be enjoyed straight, for many spirit consumers, cocktails are the main event, the raison d'etre of alcohol. Before we embark on our compendium of recipes, we offer a few general thoughts on mixing cocktails that will enhance your efforts:

In many of the recipes, we've named a specific brand of alcohol, either because it's a proprietary blend, such as Campari or Kahlúa, or because of our personal preference. In the case of the latter, feel free to substitute your favorite brand, which may just be the brand you happen to have on hand.

Regarding the use of Cointreau, Grand Marnier, and other orange-based liqueurs, easily the most used type of liqueur at the bar, we are well aware of the inflated price of some of these brands, especially Cointreau. Therefore, in some cases, such as for the Margarita, we simply call for an orange-based liqueur. In certain cases, where a particular proprietary brand is traditional, we call for it by name. We do recommend investing in good-quality orange liqueurs such as Cointreau, Grand Marnier, or Gran Torres Orange Liqueur. As with any other ingredient, the better the quality, the better the drink.

While we think the proportions in the recipes here are correct, don't be afraid to improvise. Perhaps you like your drink a little stronger or weaker. Feel free to alter the amounts, but remember, moderate drinking should mean fewer drinks, not weaker ones.

As for the liquor called for, many of the drinks would be excellent if one spirit was substituted for another. Again, these recipes are not carved in stone. They are very forgiving, but use common sense, especially if you're serving others. Make sure you test any radical improvisations before serving them to your guests.

Remember that, with very few exceptions, cocktails should be served very cold. Avoid making a drink so large that it's warm before it can be consumed. Keep your martini glasses in the freezer or refrigerator so they're chilled when you need them.

In the recipes, we've listed the main liquor first, except where the drink is built in such a way that the ingredients are added in a specific order, in which case we list the ingredients in the order they should be added.

overheard *The trouble with jogging is that the ice falls out of your glass.*
—Martin Mull

THE MARTINI

In his delightful paean *The Martini* (Chronicle Books, 1995), author and spirits authority Barnaby Conrad III wrote that for him "the Dry Martini remains an American symbol of elusive perfection, a kind of pagan Holy Grail. The dedicated Martini drinker views this deceptively simple cocktail as a true, if fleeting, salvation, a chance to savor the best possible moment before war, bankruptcy, or time itself takes it all away." Gin, and increasingly vodka, is the very soul of a Martini, the essence by which those fleeting moments of salvation can be enjoyed.

The modern obsession with "dry" Martinis, however, leads us to reconsider the Martini, surely the most famous cocktail and, in one form or another, one of the oldest. Much has been written about this libation, humorously and otherwise, usually waxing poetic about its ability to soothe away life's troubles, especially for the beleaguered businessman. (There have probably been more *New Yorker* cartoons involving the Martini than almost any other subject.) Often, the subject centers on the degree of dryness to which a proper Martini should be taken. Not counting the olive, which is optional, there are three components to a Martini; listed in the order they should go into the mixing glass, they are ice, dry vermouth, and gin or vodka. How and in what amounts these ingredients are used determines how wet or dry any given Martini will be. With that in mind, we'll consider each ingredient separately.

ICE

A Martini, or any good cocktail, should be cold, but the ice is more than merely a means of chilling your gin (if you just want cold liquor, keep it in the freezer). When shaken thoroughly, approximately eight to ten seconds vigorously, some of the ice will melt and that water becomes a part of the drink. Specifically, if you use two and a half ounces of liquor and a splash of vermouth, after mixing the drink you should be left with approximately four ounces of cocktail. Again, if you prefer your spirit undiluted, simply keep it in the freezer and pour directly into the glass.

VERMOUTH

The original recipes for the Martini called for as much as two parts vermouth to three parts gin, and sometimes even more. Of course, tastes have changed considerably since that time and the Martini has evolved toward a drier drink, with some Martini lovers omitting the vermouth altogether. Bartenders use various methods and accoutrements to produce their dry Martinis, including eye droppers and atomizers. Winston Churchill is said to have mixed his Martinis while looking across the room at a bottle of vermouth. Not dry enough? In the popular 1970s television show *M*A*S*H*, Alan Alda's character, Hawkeye, recommends shaking the Martini while looking at a picture of the inventor of vermouth! Sir Winston would no doubt have been amused.

We think all this discrimination against vermouth is a mistake, and that vermouth should be used in a Martini, albeit sparingly. It lends a certain bouquet to the drink, especially when vodka is involved, although Olivier maintains that we still put vermouth in a Martini simply because of tradition. In any case, we advocate two methods of achieving a dry Martini: Olivier likes to rinse a cold glass with vermouth before mixing, in which case you might want to keep your vermouth in the refrigerator so as not to warm the glass. James prefers to put a splash of vermouth directly into the ice in the mixing glass before adding the liquor of choice, which we hope at least once in your life will be gin. We both use Noilly Prat dry vermouth.

GIN

A Vodka Martini can be a lovely thing, and depending on the brand of vodka used, it can be a libation worthy of the exalted name. Gin, however, lifts this classic into the realm of the divine and makes it a serious drink for serious drinkers. Depending on your brand, the botanicals infused into the gin, enhanced ever so slightly by the several dozen more flavorings found in good vermouth, supply layer upon layer of flavor and satisfaction. Almost any decent brand of gin will make a good Martini. Some are happy with inexpensive, domestic brands (Julia Child, ever the proletarian, drank Gordon's), while others want nothing less than top-shelf names, like Beefeater, Boodles, Tanqueray, Bombay, or Bombay Sapphire.

We encourage you to taste as many brands as possible of both gin and vodka at your local watering hole until you arrive at your favorite.

Garnish Though a garnish is optional, the traditional garnish for a Martini is, of course, the olive, but also acceptable even to purists are a twist of lemon or a cocktail onion (whereupon the drink becomes a Gibson). Don't use gourmet olives, marinated in olive oil and herbs, unless of course you want your Martini to taste like that. Martini olives should be packed in brine, not oil, or you will have an oil slick atop your cocktail. The most common and most popular are pitted and stuffed with a slice of pimiento. This has more to do with tradition than taste—the pimiento primarily adds color. If using a twist of lemon, make the twist with a stripper or channel knife directly over the drink. This method will produce a spritz of essential oils that will do more to flavor the drink than a dried-out lemon peel, no matter how much you manhandle it.

SHAKEN OR STIRRED?

James Bond's famous admonition that he preferred his Martinis shaken, not stirred has caused consternation and debate ever since. W. Somerset Maugham advised to stir "so that the molecules lie sensuously on top of one another." Others warn that too rough a treatment will "bruise" the gin. Hmm. We think you can bruise an apple, bruise your shin, and even bruise your ego, but we have never been convinced that you can bruise gin. Although you can make a good Martini by either method, the principal objective should be to make sure the drink is very cold and well mixed. Therefore, we go with Bond on this one and recommend shaking your Martinis, as this is the best and easiest way to ensure your Martini will be the proper temperature.

Alcoholic drinks contain calories but don't contribute to weight gain, according to extensive medical research. This may be due to the fact that alcohol is processed in the body with greater ease than sugars, fats, and proteins, and that alcohol energy is not efficiently used. Also, alcohol seems to increase the metabolism, causing calories to be burned rather than stored in the body as fat. Studies also show that as alcohol consumption increases, the consumption of sugar tends to go down. As to the great American "beer belly," it's the chicken wings, not the beer.

A MARTINI IS A MARTINI IS A MARTINI

When does a Martini cease to be a Martini? In the past few years, Martini menus have become all the rage, with bars offering sometimes dozens of different varieties. Apple Martinis, Midori Martinis, Cajun Martinis, and even Chocolate Martinis (see page 153) are not uncommon at all. Garnishes also vary, from caperberries to pickled tomatoes, chiles, and more. While purists may scoff at these modern aberrations of a drink many regard as sacrosanct, it is possible to look at the Martini as a canvas upon which any number of unique and seductive flavors can be applied. This is especially true when vodka is used instead of gin. Vodka, with its neutral, almost flavorless character, is a perfect base for any number of exotic flavorings. A Martini, then, is the perfect drink with which to experiment. And lest we forget, the original recipes for the Martini were based on sweet gin, sweet vermouth, and orange bitters, a far cry from the dry, austere versions considered authentic today. Perhaps in the end the Martini is, like Paris and California, a state of mind rather than a definitive, concrete thing. After all, any cocktail is an ethereal entity, a spirit, a fleeting pleasure that by its very nature lasts but a few moments. In that light, mix away and let your Martini go where the spirit—or liqueur—takes you. For the purists out there, we offer our version of a classic Martini. For the rest of you, we've included a few variations we've come to like.

Note: While we believe that by nature a Martini is made with gin, and that if vodka is opted for it should be called a "Vodka Martini," we will, for the sake of brevity, concede that all the Martini recipes included here, unless otherwise noted, can be made with either gin or vodka.

 A jury was once put on trial themselves for consuming the evidence in a bootlegging trial. Of course, they argued they were simply trying to determine if the liquid really contained alcohol. They were eventually let off but so was the bootlegger, for lack of evidence. That's some catch-22.

MARTINI

This recipe yields a dry Martini. For a downright wet Martini, combine one part vermouth to two parts gin in a shaker with ice. Shake well and strain into a chilled martini glass.

Splash of dry vermouth
2½ to 3 ounces gin or vodka
Garnish of choice

For a dry martini, pour chilled vermouth directly in the chilled glass, swirl to coat, and discard the excess. Place the gin in a shaker with ice, shake well, and strain over desired garnish into the martini glass. For a slightly less dry version, combine the vermouth and gin in a shaker with ice. Shake well and strain into a chilled martini glass.

SWEET MARTINI

This version harks back to original recipes in which Old Tom gin was called for, a sweet variety that's very difficult to find nowadays.

3 ounces gin
Splash of sweet vermouth
Dash of orange bitters
Twist of orange, for garnish

Combine the gin, vermouth, and bitters in a shaker with ice. Shake well and strain into a chilled martini glass. Garnish with the twist of orange.

APPLE MARTINI

1½ ounces vodka
½ ounce applejack or apple schnapps

Combine the vodka and applejack in a shaker with ice. Shake well and strain into a chilled martini glass.

what's in a name?

There seem to be as many theories (or myths) on the origin of the Martini—both the word and the drink—as there are about the word *cocktail*. The town of Martinez, California, actually has a monument with a brass plaque proclaiming their town as the birthplace of the famous drink. But even there the stories differ. One has it that a miner on his way to Martinez was given the drink, and the bartender named it for his destination. Another, and obviously the preferred version in Martinez, has the miner receiving the new drink in a saloon in Martinez on his way to the goldfields. The miner, incidentally, is said to have gone on to run saloons in San Francisco, introducing the drink to the rest of the world. New York also lays claim to the cocktail. There, supposedly a bartender named Martini di Arma di Taggia first crafted the drink in the bar at the Knickerbocker Hotel. Moving further east, the

APPLE MARTINI (Variation)

1½ ounces vodka
½ ounce applejack
Apple juice to fill

Combine the vodka and applejack in a shaker with ice. Shake well and strain over fresh ice in a highball glass. Fill with apple juice.

CHOCOLATE MARTINI

We've named our brands below, but you can use your favorite brand of chocolate and vanilla liqueurs. For some tasty variations, try replacing the vanilla liqueur with one of the following: crème de menthe, Mandarine Napoleon, crème de cassis, or framboise.

1 ounce vodka
1 ounce Godiva chocolate liqueur
¼ ounce vanilla schnapps

Combine all the ingredients in a shaker with ice. Shake well and strain into a chilled martini glass.

MONTGOMERY

These are served at Harry's Bar in Venice.

10 parts gin
1 part dry vermouth

Mix the ingredients in a pitcher and pour into several martini glasses. Place the glasses in the freezer until the mixture is frozen. Serve frozen so they can be sipped as they thaw.

PINK GIN

2 dashes Angostura bitters
1½ ounces gin
Twist of lemon, for garnish

Put the bitters in a chilled martini glass and swirl to coat. Put the gin in a shaker with ice. Shake well and strain into the glass. Garnish with the twist of lemon.

English too have a theory: that it is named for the Martini-Henry rifle, a weapon used by the British army in the late nineteenth century. This isn't so far-fetched when you consider another cocktail named for a military weapon, the French 75. No less an authority than the *Oxford American Dictionary* claims the drink takes its name from the Martini & Rossi brand of vermouth. This theory fails to take into account the fact that this Italian vermouth wasn't imported to the United States until long after the drink began routinely appearing in bar manuals, nor does it explain how the two spirits came to be combined in the first place. Again, except for in some spirited bar debates, it matters little for whom the Martini was invented and so named. We do, however, suggest that if you ever find yourself in Martinez, stop and raise a cold one to intrepid miners everywhere.

THE MANHATTAN

The Manhattan is perhaps the Martini's only real competition as the world's most sophisticated and elegant cocktail and, indeed, is just as famous. The great food writer James Villas once wrote, "A properly made Manhattan represents the height of the mixologist's art. The whiskey must be fine Bourbon or blended American, the vermouth must be the best sweet Italian, the bitters must be Angostura, and the proportions must be measured exactly, chilled quickly but thoroughly with large ice cubes to prevent dilution, and poured through a strainer over a stemmed maraschino cherry into a chilled 4- to 6-ounce cocktail glass." We couldn't have put it better ourselves, and while we don't join Mr. Villas in deriding the Martini as "a pretty crass drink," we do believe the Manhattan to be the equal of the Martini and that it should be accorded the same respect. Unlike the Martini, the recipe for a Manhattan is generally agreed upon, with the exception perhaps of the choice in whiskey. Many recipes insist it should be made with blended whiskey, or even Canadian whisky. Although one can certainly make a fine Manhattan with either of those, we think it's even better made with good bourbon. Here, then, is our version of a Manhattan, followed by a couple of variations.

what's in a name?

As to the origins of this noble cocktail, there remains little doubt that it was named for the Manhattan Club in New York City, but just why and for whom remains a matter of historical speculation. The popular theory insists it was created at a banquet held for newly elected Governor Samuel J. Tilden in 1874. The banquet was supposedly hosted by Lady (Jenny Jerome) Randolph Churchill, mother of Sir Winston, who at one time lived at the club. The hole in this theory is that Jenny Churchill gave birth to little Winston in November of that year in England, making it extremely unlikely she was at the dinner. Another story has it the dinner was for New York Supreme Court Judge Charles Henry Truax in

MANHATTAN

*For a dry Manhattan, substitute dry ver-
mouth for the sweet; a twist of lemon is
the traditional garnish. For a Perfect Manhattan, substitute dry vermouth for half
of the sweet vermouth and garnish with
either a twist of lemon or a maraschino
cherry, as you prefer.*

1½ ounces whiskey,
  preferably bourbon
¾ ounce sweet vermouth
2 dashes Angostura bitters
Maraschino cherry, for garnish

Combine the whiskey, vermouth, and
bitters in a shaker with ice. Stir well
and strain over the cherry in a chilled
martini glass.

CUBAN MANHATTAN

1½ ounces amber rum
  (we prefer Flor de Caña)
¾ ounce sweet vermouth
Maraschino cherry, for garnish

Combine the rum and vermouth in
a shaker with ice. Stir well and strain
over the cherry in a chilled martini
glass.

PARISIAN MANHATTAN

1½ ounces blended whiskey
½ ounce sweet vermouth
¼ ounce Amer Picon
Maraschino cherry, for garnish

Combine the whiskey, vermouth, and
Amer Picon in a shaker with ice. Stir
well and strain over the cherry in a
chilled martini glass.

about 1890 and that, again, Lady Churchill was in attendance. In his delightful essay on the Manhattan, James Villas cites the judge's daughter, Carol Truax, on her version of the genesis of the drink. She maintains that her corpulent father, then president of the club, was ordered by his doctor to give up Martinis. He obeyed by concocting another drink, the Manhattan. It apparently had nothing to do with the banquet, and much to his doctor's dismay, the new drink contained even more calories than the Martini. An ironic side note is that regardless of Lady Churchill's connection to the Manhattan, Sir Winston would go on to become an avid Martini drinker.

COCKTAIL COMPENDIUM

We present here almost one hundred cocktails that we believe provide a broad range of drinks, both stylistically and in the assortment of spirits called for. They also represent, based on our many years of experience behind the bar, many of the most popular and delicious cocktails and could well provide a lifetime's worth of enjoyment.

COCKTAIL RECIPES

ABSOLUT REDHEAD

1½ ounces Absolut Pepper vodka
½ ounce freshly squeezed lime juice
½ ounce grenadine

Combine all the ingredients in a shaker with ice. Shake well and strain over fresh ice in an old-fashioned glass.

Variation: Try using different syrups such as passion fruit or berry.

ALABAMA SLAMMER

1½ ounces amaretto
1 ounce Southern Comfort
½ ounce sloe gin
1 ounce freshly squeezed lemon juice

Combine all the ingredients in a shaker with ice. Shake well and strain over fresh ice in an old-fashioned glass.

AMARETTO COOLER

1 ounce amaretto
1 ounce cranberry juice
1 ounce freshly squeezed orange juice
½ ounce freshly squeezed lime juice
Club soda to fill

Pour the amaretto and juices over ice in a highball glass. Fill with club soda. Stir.

Bacchus hath drowned more men than Neptune.
—Dr. Thomas Fuller

AMARETTO SOUR

1½ ounces amaretto
½ ounce freshly squeezed lemon juice
1 teaspoon superfine sugar
Maraschino cherry, for garnish

Combine the amaretto, lemon juice, and sugar in a shaker with ice. Shake well and strain over the cherry in a chilled martini glass.

AMERICANO

1 ounce Campari
1 ounce sweet vermouth
Club soda to fill
Twist of orange, for garnish

Pour the Campari and vermouth over ice in a highball glass. Fill with club soda. Garnish with the twist of orange.

Variation: In Europe this is served in a rocks glass with no soda and a few drops of gin floated on top.

ANDALUSIA

¾ ounce light rum
¾ ounce brandy (preferably Spanish)
¾ ounce dry sherry (such as fino or manzanilla)
Dash of Angostura bitters

Combine all the ingredients in a shaker with ice. Shake well and strain into a chilled martini glass.

Variation: For a sweeter version, use a sweet sherry and garnish with an orange twist.

APRICOT COOLER

1 ounce apricot brandy
½ ounce orange juice
½ ounce freshly squeezed lime juice
Dash of simple syrup
Club soda to fill

Pour the brandy, orange juice, lime juice, and syrup over ice in a highball glass. Fill with club soda. Stir.

APRICOT SOUR

1 ounce apricot brandy
½ ounce freshly squeezed orange juice
½ ounce freshly squeezed lime juice
Dash of simple syrup or 1 teaspoon
   sugar
Maraschino cherry, for garnish

Combine the brandy, orange juice, lime juice, and simple syrup in a shaker with ice. Shake well and strain over the cherry in a chilled martini glass.

Variation: Add dimension with 1/2 ounce of orange juice.

ARNAUD

1½ ounces gin
½ ounce sweet vermouth
Dash of cassis
Twist of lemon, for garnish

Combine the gin, vermouth, and cassis in a shaker with ice. Shake well and strain over fresh ice in an old-fashioned glass. Garnish with the twist of lemon.

AVIATION

1½ ounces gin
½ ounce maraschino liqueur
½ ounce freshly squeezed lemon juice

Combine all the ingredients in a shaker with ice. Shake well and strain into a chilled martini glass.

B-52

Both the B-52 and the B-54 were originally meant to be layered drinks, carefully poured into a small glass. We prefer them on the rocks but layer them nonetheless. Even with ice cubes in the glass they're still arresting to look at, and any way you serve them they're very tasty.

¾ ounce Kahlúa
¾ ounce Baileys Irish Cream
¾ ounce Grand Marnier

Pour the Kahlúa over ice in an old-fashioned glass. Carefully pour in the Baileys and then the Grand Marnier over the back of a spoon so that the liqueurs stay in distinct layers (see page 140). Let the consumer do the stirring.

B-54

¾ ounce amaretto
¾ ounce Kahlúa
¾ ounce Baileys Irish Cream

Pour the amaretto over ice in an old-fashioned glass. Carefully pour in the Kahlúa and then the Baileys over the back of a spoon so that the liqueurs stay in distinct layers (see page 140). Let the consumer do the stirring.

BEAUTIFUL

1 ounce Cognac
½ ounce Grand Marnier

Heat a brandy snifter by pouring in hot water, swirling, then discarding the water. Pour in the Cognac and Grand Marnier and serve.

BERRY CAIPIRINHA

1 lime, cut into 8 wedges
½ teaspoon sugar
1 ounce Chambord
1½ ounces cachaça or light rum
Crushed ice

Place the lime pieces, sugar, and Chambord in an old-fashioned glass and muddle thoroughly. Add the cachaça and stir to mix. Fill with crushed ice.

BLOODY MARY

(see page 162)

BRANDY ALEXANDER

1½ ounces brandy
 (preferably VSOP Cognac)
½ ounce crème de cacao or other chocolate liqueur
1 ounce heavy cream
Freshly ground nutmeg, for garnish

Combine the brandy, liqueur, and cream in a shaker with ice. Shake well and strain into a chilled martini glass and sprinkle with the nutmeg.

BRANDY FLIP

A flip can be made with almost any spirit, although brandy seems to work best. They are so called because they were originally poured back and forth between two mixing glasses, creating a frothy, foamy drink. Shaking works just as well.

1½ ounces brandy
 (preferably VSOP Cognac)
1 ounce heavy cream
½ ounce simple syrup
Freshly ground nutmeg, for garnish

Combine the brandy, cream, and syrup in a shaker with ice. Shake well and strain into a chilled martini glass and sprinkle with the nutmeg.

BRANDY SMASH

4 to 6 mint leaves
1 teaspoon sugar
2½ ounces brandy

Put the mint leaves and sugar in an old-fashioned glass with a tiny splash of the brandy. Muddle well to crush the leaves and dissolve the sugar. Fill the glass with ice and pour in the rest of the brandy.

BRAVE BULL

2 ounces tequila
1 ounce Kahlúa

Pour the tequila and Kahlúa over ice in an old-fashioned glass and stir.

BULL SHOT

1½ ounces vodka
4 ounces beef bouillon or beef
   consommé
1 teaspoon freshly squeezed lemon juice
1 or 2 dashes of Worcestershire sauce
Dash of Tabasco sauce
Pinch of celery salt
½ teaspoon horseradish (optional)
Freshly ground black pepper
Wedge of lemon, for garnish

Combine the vodka, bouillon, lemon juice, Worcestershire sauce, Tabasco sauce, celery salt, and horseradish in a shaker with ice. Shake well and strain over fresh ice in a highball glass. Garnish with freshly ground black pepper and the lemon wedge.

CAIPIRINHA

If you can't find cachaça, use light rum.

1 lime, cut into 8 wedges
4 sugar cubes, or 2 heaping teaspoons
   sugar
2 ounces cachaça
Crushed ice

Place the lime wedges and the sugar in an old-fashioned glass. Crush the lime to release its juice, and muddle to dissolve the sugar and blend it with the lime. Pour in the cachaça and stir to dissolve the sugar completely. Top with crushed ice.

CAPE CODDER

1½ ounces vodka
Cranberry juice to fill
Wedge of lime, for garnish

Pour the vodka over ice in a highball glass. Fill with cranberry juice. Garnish with the lime wedge.

CLASSIC CHAMPAGNE COCKTAIL

1 sugar cube
2 dashes Angostura bitters
Champagne to fill
Twist of lemon, for garnish

Place the sugar cube in a champagne flute. Add the bitters on top of the sugar. Fill with good Champagne. Garnish with the twist of lemon.

COFFEE COOLER

1½ ounces vodka
1 ounce Kahlúa
1 ounce heavy cream
Cold strong black coffee to fill
1 small scoop coffee or vanilla ice cream

Pour the vodka, Kahlúa, and cream into an old-fashioned glass without ice. Pour in cold coffee to almost fill and top with the ice cream.

BLOODY MARY

2 ounces vodka
5 ounces tomato juice
½ ounce freshly squeezed lemon juice
2 to 3 dashes Worcestershire sauce
½ teaspoon horseradish
⅛ teaspoon celery seed or a pinch of
celery salt
⅛ teaspoon freshly ground black pepper
1 to 2 dashes Tabasco sauce
1 stalk celery
Wedge of lime, for garnish

Combine the vodka, tomato juice,
lemon juice, Worcestershire sauce,
horseradish, celery seed, pepper, and
Tabasco sauce in a shaker with ice.
Shake well and strain over fresh ice in
a highball glass. Place the celery stalk
in the glass like a swizzle stick. Garnish
with a freshly ground pepper and the
lime wedge.

VARIATIONS

- Substitute whiskey for vodka

- Add ½ ounce sweet sherry

- Use freshly grated ginger instead of
horseradish

- Substitute gin and grainy mustard for
vodka and horse radish

- Substitute tequila and chopped
jalapeños for vodka and horseradish

TOMATO JUICE (COOKED)

Makes approximately 1 quart

12 medium-sized, ripe tomatoes,
quartered
1 yellow onion, quartered
2 celery stalks with leaves, roughly
chopped
½ bay leaf
3 sprigs parsley
Juice of half lemon
¼ teaspoon paprika
¼ teaspoon sugar
Salt and freshly ground black pepper
to taste

Combine tomatoes, onion, celery, bay
leaf and parsley in a soup pot over
medium-high heat. Simmer for ½
hour. Strain entire contents through
a food mill, retaining only the juice.
Season with the lemon juice, paprika,
sugar, salt and pepper.

Chill and serve.

TOMATO JUICE (RAW)

12 medium-sized, ripe tomatoes,
quartered
Salt and freshly ground black pepper
to taste
Juice of half lemon

Blend the ripe tomatoes in a blender
or food processor until smooth. Season
with salt, pepper, and lemon juice.

Chill and serve.

COLLINS (see Tom Collins)

COSMOPOLITAN

We recommend using good orange-flavored vodka like Absolut Mandrin or Hangar One Mandarin Blossom.

1½ ounces vodka
½ ounce Cointreau
½ ounce freshly squeezed lime juice
½ ounce cranberry juice
Slice of lime, for garnish

Combine the vodka, Cointreau, lime juice, and cranberry juice in a shaker with ice. Shake well and strain into a chilled martini glass. Garnish with the lime slice.

COUNT STROGANOFF

1½ ounces vodka
¾ ounce white crème de cacao
½ ounce freshly squeezed lemon juice
Crushed ice

Combine all the ingredients in a shaker with crushed ice. Shake well and strain into a chilled martini glass.

CUBA LIBRE

1½ ounces light rum
Cola to fill
2 wedges of lime

Pour the rum over ice in a highball glass. Fill with cola. Squeeze one lime wedge over the drink and drop it into the glass. Garnish with the other lime wedge.

DAIQUIRI

Superfine sugar, for coating rim (optional)
1½ ounces light rum
Juice of ½ lime
½ teaspoon sugar
Slice of lime, for garnish

Coat the rim of a chilled martini glass with sugar. Combine the rum, lime juice, and sugar in a shaker with ice. Shake well and strain into the glass. Garnish with the lime slice.

DIRTY GIRL SCOUT

1 ounce Baileys Irish Cream
1 ounce Kahlúa
1 ounce vodka
Splash of green crème de menthe

Combine all the ingredients in a shaker with ice. Shake well and strain over fresh ice in an old-fashioned glass.

DUBONNET COCKTAIL

1½ ounces Dubonnet Rouge
1 ounce gin
Twist of lemon, for garnish

Combine the Dubonnet and gin in a shaker with ice and stir. Strain into a chilled martini glass and garnish with the twist of lemon.

DUBONNET FIZZ

3 ounces Dubonnet Rouge
1 ounce vodka
Club soda to fill
Twist of lemon, for garnish

Combine the Dubonnet and vodka in a shaker with ice. Shake well and strain over fresh ice in a highball glass. Fill with club soda and garnish with the twist of lemon.

EL BURRO

1 ounce Kahlúa
1 ounce dark rum
1 ounce coconut cream
Sprig of mint, for garnish

Combine the Kahlúa, rum, and coconut cream in a shaker with ice. Shake well and strain into a chilled martini glass. Garnish with the sprig of mint.

FRENCH CONNECTION

1 ounce Cognac
½ ounce amaretto

Heat a brandy snifter by pouring in hot water, swirling, then discarding the water. Pour in the Cognac and amaretto and serve.

FRENCH 75

¾ ounce gin
¼ ounce freshly squeezed lemon juice
Dash of grenadine
Champagne to fill

Combine the gin, lemon juice, and grenadine in a shaker with ice. Shake well and strain into a champagne flute. Fill with champagne.

FRIAR TUCK

1 ounce Frangelico
1 ounce brandy
1 ounce freshly squeezed lemon juice
Splash of grenadine
Maraschino cherry, for garnish

Combine the Frangelico, brandy, lemon juice, and grenadine in a shaker with ice. Shake well and strain over the cherry in a chilled martini glass.

GIMLET

1½ ounces gin or vodka
½ ounce freshly squeezed lemon juice
Splash of Rose's Lime Juice
Wedge of lime, for garnish

Combine the gin, lemon juice, and Rose's Lime Juice in a shaker with ice. Shake well and strain into a chilled martini glass. Garnish with the lime wedge.

GIN FIZZ

1½ ounces gin
½ ounce freshly squeezed lemon juice
Dash of simple syrup or ½ teaspoon
    superfine sugar
Club soda to fill

Combine the gin, lemon juice, and
syrup in a shaker with ice. Shake well
and strain over fresh ice in a highball
glass. Fill with club soda.

GIN RICKEY

1½ ounces gin
Juice of 1 lime, freshly squeezed
1 teaspoon superfine sugar
2 dashes Angostura bitters
Club soda to fill
Wedge of lime, for garnish

Combine the gin, lime juice, sugar,
and bitters in a shaker with ice. Shake
well and strain into a highball glass
filled with ice. Fill with club soda and
garnish with the lime wedge.

GINGER TOM COLLINS

1½ ounces gin
½ ounce ginger syrup
    (see recipe, page 129)
½ ounce freshly squeezed lime juice
Club soda to fill

Combine the gin, syrup, and lime juice
in a shaker with ice. Shake well and
strain over fresh ice in a highball or
collins glass. Fill with club soda.

GODFATHER

1½ ounces Scotch whisky
½ ounce amaretto

Combine the Scotch and amaretto in an old-fashioned glass over ice.

GODMOTHER

1½ ounces vodka
½ ounce amaretto

Combine the vodka and amaretto in an old-fashioned glass over ice.

GOLDEN DREAM

¾ ounce Galliano
¾ ounce orange-based liqueur
1 ounce freshly squeezed orange juice
½ ounce heavy cream

Combine all the ingredients in a shaker with ice. Shake well and strain into a chilled martini glass.

GRAND MIMOSA

1 ounce Grand Marnier
2 ounces freshly squeezed orange juice
Champagne, or other good quality sparkling wine to fill

Pour the Grand Marnier and orange juice into a champagne flute. Fill with good quality Champagne.

GRAPEFRUIT DAIQUIRI

1½ ounces aged rum
1 ounce freshly squeezed grapefruit juice
1 teaspoon superfine sugar

Combine all the ingredients in a shaker with ice. Shake well and strain into a chilled martini glass.

GRASSHOPPER

1 ounce green crème de menthe
1 ounce white crème de cacao
1 ounce heavy cream

Combine all the ingredients in a shaker with ice. Shake well and strain into a chilled martini glass.

GREYHOUND

1½ ounces vodka
Freshly squeezed grapefruit juice to fill

Pour the vodka over ice in a highball glass. Fill with grapefruit juice.

Variation: For a Salty Dog, simply salt the rim of the glass.

HARVEY WALLBANGER

1½ ounces vodka
Freshly squeezed orange juice to fill
½ ounce Galliano
Slice of orange, for garnish

Pour the vodka over ice in a high-ball glass. Fill almost to the top with orange juice. Pour the Galliano on top and garnish with the orange slice.

HAVANA CLUB

1½ ounces light rum
½ ounce dry vermouth
Twist of lemon, for garnish

Combine the rum and vermouth in a
shaker with ice. Shake well and strain
into a chilled martini glass. Garnish
with the twist of lemon.

HONEY BEE

This is basically a chilled Rum Toddy.

2 ounces amber rum
½ ounce freshly squeezed lemon juice
1 teaspoon honey

Combine all the ingredients in a
shaker with ice. Shake well and strain
into a chilled martini glass.

HOT TODDY

Lemon wedge
4 or 5 cloves
1½ ounces whiskey or rum
½ ounce freshly squeezed lemon juice
1 teaspoon honey
Boiling water to fill

Stud the lemon wedge with the cloves.
Combine the whiskey, lemon juice,
honey, and studded lemon wedge in
an 8-ounce heatproof glass mug with
boiling hot water.

HURRICANE

1 ounce light rum
1 ounce dark rum
½ ounce amaretto
1 ounce freshly squeezed orange juice
1 ounce pineapple juice
½ ounce freshly squeezed lime juice
Splash of passion fruit syrup
Splash of grenadine
Crushed ice
Slice of lime, for garnish

Combine the light rum, dark rum,
amaretto, orange juice, pineapple
juice, lime juice, passion fruit syrup,
and grenadine in a shaker with ice.
Shake well and strain over crushed
ice in a collins glass. Garnish with the
lime slice.

ICE PICK

1½ ounces vodka
Iced tea to fill
Wedge of lemon, for garnish

Pour the vodka over ice in a highball
glass. Fill with iced tea and garnish
with the lemon wedge.

IRISH COFFEE

1 sugar cube
1½ ounces Irish whiskey
Dash of Cointreau
Strong hot black coffee to fill
Whipped cream, for topping

Put the sugar cube in a heatproof glass
mug. Add the whiskey and Cointreau.
Pour in hot coffee to almost fill and
top with whipped cream.

It pays to drink alcohol. According to the national Household Survey on Drug Abuse by the U.S. Department of Health and Human Services, men in the United States who drink alcohol receive about 7 percent higher wages than those men who abstain. On average, women who drink receive about 3.5 percent higher wages than abstainers. Note that whether they drink or not, women still get less pay than men.

JACK ROSE

1½ ounces Calvados
½ ounce freshly squeezed lemon juice
1 teaspoon grenadine

Combine all the ingredients in a shaker with ice. Shake well and strain into a chilled martini glass.

KIR ROYALE

Champagne
Splash of crème de cassis

Fill a champagne flute almost to the top with good Champagne. Add a splash of cassis.

KURANT CASSIS

1½ ounces Absolut Kurant vodka
½ ounce crème de cassis
4 ounces freshly squeezed grapefruit juice

Pour the vodka and cassis over ice in a highball glass. Add the grapefruit juice and stir.

LEMON DROP

There are several good brands of lemon-infused vodka. Our favorites are Ketel One Citroen and Hangar One Buddha's Hand.

Superfine sugar, for coating rim
1½ ounces lemon-infused vodka
¾ ounce Cointreau
½ ounce freshly squeezed lemon juice
Twist of lemon, for garnish

Coat the rim of a chilled martini glass with sugar. Combine the vodka, Cointreau, and lemon juice in a shaker with ice. Shake well and strain into the martini glass. Garnish with a long twist of lemon.

LEMONADE (nonalcoholic)

1 ounce freshly squeezed lemon juice
2 teaspoons sugar
Club soda or water to fill

Combine the lemon juice and sugar in a highball glass and stir to dissolve. Fill three-quarters full with ice, then fill with club soda.

MAI TAI

1 ounce light rum
1 ounce amber rum
½ ounce orange-based liqueur
½ ounce amaretto, or dash of orgeat
   (almond-flavored syrup)
½ ounce freshly squeezed lime juice
Dash of grenadine
Crushed ice
Slice of pineapple, for garnish
Maraschino cherry, for garnish
½ ounce dark rum, to float (optional)

Combine the light rum, amber rum, orange liqueur, amaretto, lime juice, and grenadine in a shaker with ice. Shake well and strain over crushed ice in an old-fashioned glass. Garnish with the pineapple slice and cherry.

MANHATTAN AND VARIATIONS
(see pages 154–155)

MARGARITA

Kosher salt, for coating rim
1½ ounces tequila
½ ounce orange-based liqueur
Juice of ½ lime
Slice of lime, for garnish

Coat the rim of either a chilled martini glass (for straight up) or an old-fashioned glass (for on the rocks) with salt. Combine the tequila, orange liqueur, and lime juice in a shaker with ice. Shake well and strain into the glass (over ice in the old-fashioned glass). Garnish with the lime slice.

MARTINI AND VARIATIONS
(see pages 152–153)

MEXICAN COFFEE

1 ounce tequila
¾ ounce Kahlúa
Strong hot black coffee to fill
Whipped cream, for topping

Pour the tequila and Kahlúa into a heatproof glass mug. Pour in hot coffee to almost fill and top with whipped cream.

MINT CONDITION

1½ ounces light rum
½ ounce peppermint schnapps
1 ounce guava, mango, or papaya juice
   or nectar
Dash of grenadine

Combine all the ingredients in a shaker with ice. Shake well and strain over fresh ice in an old-fashioned glass.

MINT JULEP

6 to 8 mint leaves
1 teaspoon sugar
1½ ounces bourbon
Crushed ice
2 to 3 sprigs of mint, for garnish

Combine the mint, sugar, and a tiny bit of the bourbon in the bottom of an old-fashioned glass. Muddle to dissolve the sugar and crush the mint. Add the remaining bourbon. Fill with crushed ice and garnish with a few mint sprigs.

MOJITO

8 to 10 mint leaves
Juice of ½ lime
1½ teaspoons superfine sugar
2 ounces light rum
Club soda to fill

Combine the mint leaves, lime juice, and sugar in a highball glass. Crush the leaves, either with a muddler or the back of a spoon. Add the rum and stir to dissolve the sugar completely. Fill the glass with ice and add club soda to fill.

MOSCOW MULE

1½ ounces vodka
½ ounce freshly squeezed lime juice
Ginger beer or ginger ale to fill
Wedge of lime, for garnish

Pour the vodka and lime juice over ice in a highball glass. Fill with ginger beer and garnish with the lime wedge.

MUDSLIDE

¾ ounce vodka
¾ ounce Baileys Irish Cream
¾ ounce Kahlúa

Pour the vodka, Baileys, and Kahlúa over ice in an old-fashioned glass.

NEGRONI

1 ounce gin
¾ ounce Campari
¾ ounce sweet vermouth
Twist of orange, for garnish

Combine the gin, Campari, and vermouth in a shaker with ice. Shake well and strain into a martini glass. Garnish with the twist of orange.

OLD-FASHIONED

½ teaspoon superfine sugar, or 1 sugar cube
2 dashes Angostura bitters
½ orange slice
Maraschino cherry
1½ ounces whiskey
   (either blended whiskey or bourbon)
Club soda to fill

Place the sugar in an old-fashioned glass and shake the bitters on top of it. Add the orange slice and cherry and mash strongly with a muddler or the back of a spoon. Add the whiskey, fill with ice, then fill with club soda.

OPERA

1 ounce gin
½ ounce Dubonnet Rouge
Dash of maraschino liqueur
Twist of orange, for garnish

Combine the gin, Dubonnet, and maraschino liqueur in a shaker with ice. Shake well and strain into a chilled martini glass. Garnish with orange twist.

THE OTHER APPLE

1½ ounces Calvados
1 ounce freshly squeezed grapefruit
juice

Combine the Calvados and grapefruit
juice in a shaker with ice. Shake well
and strain into a chilled martini glass.

PARISIAN

1½ ounces gin
¾ ounce Noilly Prat dry vermouth
Dash of crème de cassis
Twist of lemon, for garnish

Combine the gin, vermouth, and
cassis in a shaker with ice. Shake well
and strain into a chilled martini glass.
Garnish with the twist of lemon.

PEACH FUZZ

1½ ounces peach brandy
½ ounce white crème de cacao
½ ounce apple schnapps
1 ounce heavy cream

Combine all the ingredients in a
shaker with ice. Shake well and strain
into a chilled martini glass.

PERROQUET

French for parrot, *this is a popular aperitif in the south of France. If you replace
the syrup with grenadine it's called a
Tomate, with orgeat (almond) syrup it's
called a Maurresque ("Moor").*

1 ounce pastis
½ ounce mint syrup (see page 129)

Pour the pastis and syrup over a few ice
cubes in an old-fashioned glass. Serve
a small pitcher of ice-cold water on the
side for the consumer to add as desired.

PINK LADY

1½ ounces gin
½ ounce lemon juice
1 teaspoon superfine sugar
Splash of grenadine

Combine ingredients in a shaker with
ice. Shake well and strain into a chilled
martini glass.

PLANTATION PUNCH

1½ ounces dark or amber rum
¾ ounce Southern Comfort
2 ounces freshly squeezed orange juice
2 ounces pineapple, guava, or
cranberry juice
1 ounce freshly squeezed lemon juice
Dash of grenadine
Club soda to fill
Slice of orange, for garnish

Combine the rum, Southern Comfort,
orange juice, pineapple juice, lemon
juice, and grenadine in a shaker with
ice. Shake well and strain over fresh ice
in a collins glass. Fill with club soda
and garnish with the orange slice.

RED CAIPIROSHKA

Our choice of vodka here is Hangar One Kaffir Lime.

1½ ounces lime-flavored vodka
Dash of crème de cassis
½ ounce freshly squeezed lime juice
8 blackberries
Crushed ice
Powdered sugar, for garnish (optional)

Combine the vodka, cassis, lime juice, and blackberries in an old-fashioned glass. Muddle thoroughly. Fill with crushed ice and dust with the powdered sugar.

ROLLS ROYCE

1½ ounces gin
½ ounce dry vermouth
½ ounce sweet vermouth
Splash of Bénédictine
Maraschino cherry, for garnish

Combine the gin, sweet vermouth, dry vermouth, and Bénédictine in a shaker with ice. Shake well and strain over the cherry in a chilled martini glass.

RUSTY NAIL

1 ounce Scotch whisky
½ ounce Drambuie

Pour the Scotch and then the Drambuie over ice in an old-fashioned glass.

SALTY DOG

(see page 167)

SAZERAC

Splash of pastis
2 ounces bourbon
2 dashes Angostura bitters
½ teaspoon superfine sugar
Twist of lemon, for garnish

Pour a splash of pastis into a chilled martini glass and swirl to coat. Combine the bourbon, bitters, and sugar in a shaker with ice. Shake well and strain into the glass. Garnish with the twist of lemon.

SCREWDRIVER

1½ ounces vodka
Freshly squeezed orange juice to fill

Pour the vodka over ice in a highball glass. Fill with orange juice.

SEA BREEZE

1½ ounces vodka
Freshly squeezed grapefruit juice
Cranberry juice

Pour the vodka over ice in a highball glass. Fill with equal parts grapefruit juice and cranberry juice.

SHIRLEY TEMPLE (nonalcoholic)

We recommend making lemonade from scratch for this drink, but you can use any good lemon soda, such as 7 Up.

Sparkling lemonade or bottled lemon
  soda
Dash of grenadine
3 maraschino cherries, for garnish

Pour the lemonade over ice in a highball glass. Add a dash of grenadine and garnish with the maraschino cherries.

SIDECAR

Superfine sugar, for coating rim
  (optional)
1½ ounces brandy
½ ounce Cointreau or triple sec
¾ ounce freshly squeezed lemon juice
Twist of lemon, for garnish

Coat the rim of a chilled martini glass with sugar. Combine the brandy, Cointreau, and lemon juice in a shaker with ice. Shake moderately and strain into the glass. Garnish with the twist of lemon.

SINGAPORE SLING

1½ ounces gin
½ ounce cherry brandy
½ ounce freshly squeezed lemon juice
Club soda to fill
Maraschino cherry, for garnish

Combine the gin, brandy, and lemon juice in a shaker with ice. Shake well and strain over fresh ice in a collins glass. Fill with club soda and garnish with the cherry.

SLEEPY TODDY

1 ounce rum
1 chamomile tea bag
1 teaspoon honey
Wedge of lemon, for garnish

Combine the rum, tea bag, and honey in a 8-ounce heatproof glass mug. Pour in boiling hot water. Let steep for 3 minutes, then serve with the lemon wedge.

SLOW BURNER

1 ounce aged, dark rum
½ ounce Kahlúa
½ ounce peppermint schnapps

Combine all the ingredients in a brandy snifter.

STINGER

1½ ounces brandy
½ ounce crème de menthe

Pour the brandy and crème de menthe over ice in an old-fashioned glass. Stir.

STINGER SOUR

We like this one served straight up, but it works fine on the rocks as well.

1½ ounces bourbon
½ ounce peppermint schnapps
½ ounce freshly squeezed lemon juice

Combine all the ingredients in a shaker with crushed ice. Shake well and strain into a chilled martini glass or, if you prefer, over fresh ice in an old-fashioned glass.

TEQUILA SUNRISE

1½ ounces tequila
Freshly squeezed orange juice to fill
½ ounce grenadine

Pour the tequila over ice in a highball glass. Fill with orange juice almost to the top. Add the grenadine. Do not stir.

TOASTED ALMOND

1½ ounces amaretto
1 ounce Kahlúa
2 ounces heavy cream
Unsweetened cocoa powder, for garnish
Toasted slivered almond, for garnish
  (optional)

Combine the amaretto, Kahlúa, and cream in a shaker with ice. Shake well and strain into a chilled martini glass. Sprinkle with the cocoa and almonds.

TOM COLLINS

This is the basic recipe for any type of Collins. All you need to do is substitute your spirit of choice, such as brandy, rum, vodka, or any kind of whiskey, for the gin.

1½ ounces gin
1 ounce freshly squeezed lemon juice
1 teaspoon superfine sugar
Club soda to fill
Slice of lemon, for garnish
Maraschino cherry for garnish

Combine the gin, lemon juice, and sugar in a shaker with ice. Stir or shake gently. Strain into a collins or highball glass over fresh ice. Fill with club soda and garnish with the lemon slice and cherry.

WHISKEY SOUR

*Like a Collins, a sour can be made with
any type of liquor following this basic
recipe and substituting your spirit of
choice for the whiskey. Go easy on the
lemon and sugar.*

1½ ounces bourbon or other whiskey
½ ounce freshly squeezed lemon juice
½ teaspoon superfine sugar
Maraschino cherry, for garnish

Combine the whiskey, lemon juice,
and sugar in a shaker with ice. Shake
moderately and strain over the cherry
in a chilled martini glass.

WHITE BURNER

1½ ounces aged rum
½ ounce Kahlúa
½ ounce peppermint schnapps
½ ounce heavy cream

Combine the rum, Kahlúa, and
schnapps over ice in an old-fashioned
glass. Gently float the cream over the
top. Do not stir.

WHITE LADY

1½ ounces gin
¾ ounce Cointreau
Juice of ½ lemon

Combine all the ingredients in a
shaker with ice. Shake well and strain
into a chilled martini glass.

WHITE RUSSIAN

*Make this a Black Russian by omitting
the cream.*

1 ounce vodka
¾ ounce Kahlúa
1 ounce heavy cream or half-and-half

Pour the vodka and Kahlúa over ice
in an old-fashioned glass. Gently float
the cream over the top. Do not stir.

ZOMBIE

*For fun, soak a sugar cube with 151-proof
rum and place it on an orange slice atop
the drink. Light it on fire to serve.*

1½ ounces light rum
1½ ounces dark rum
½ ounce Cointreau
1 ounce pineapple juice
1 ounce freshly squeezed orange juice
½ ounce freshly squeezed lime juice
½ teaspoon sugar
1 teaspoon 151-proof rum
Slice of orange, for garnish
Slice of pineapple, for garnish

Combine the light rum, dark rum,
Cointreau, pineapple juice, orange
juice, lime juice, and sugar in a shaker
with ice. Shake well and strain over
fresh ice in a highball glass. Float the
151-proof rum on top. Garnish with
the pineapple and orange slices.

DRINK MACHINE

PRIMARY ALCOHOL

ALC 1
OFF VOD GIN
BEER — TEQ
— RUM
WINE
CHAM BRDY BOURB SCOT

2
1.5
1
0.5
(OZ.)

ALC 2
OFF VOD GIN
BEER — TEQ
— RUM
WINE
CHAM BRDY BOURB SCH

2
1.5
1
0.5
(OZ.)

ALC 3
OFF VOD GIN
BEER — TEQ
— RUM
WINE
CHAM BRDY BOURB SCH

2
1.5
1
0.5
(OZ.)

SWEET

SUGAR
SYRUP
LIQUEUR
OFF

Liqueur 1
OFF COINT KAHIÚA
APPLE CASSI
IRISH CRM PEACH
GRAN-M APR
MINT CHO VAN

2
1.5
1
0.5
(OZ.)

Liqueur 2
OFF COINT ROSES
APPLE CASSI
GRAN PCH
LEMON APR
MINT CHO VAN

2
1.5
1
0.5
(OZ.)

Sugar
SIMPLE SYRUP
FRUIT SYRUP
SUGAR
OFF

2
1.5
1
0.5
(OZ.)

SODA/FRUIT JUICE

FRUIT
COLA
LEMONADE
PLAIN
OFF

QTY
Fill
4
3
Splash
(OZ.)

Fruit Juice
OFF LEMON LIME
TOMA PEACH
APRI CRAN
PEAR COCO
APPLE BERRIES BANA

With the help of our friend and nuclear physicist Ed Morse, Olivier devised this machine (part Jules Verne and part Rube Goldberg) to help explain the mechanics of a cocktail… or maybe he just has too much time on his hands.

OTHER

Hot

COFFEE — Fill
WATER — 4
TEA — 3
OFF — Splash
(OZ.)

Cream

Fill
2
1.5
1
0.5
OFF
(OZ.)

Spice

GINGER — Fill
CINAMON — 2
NUTMEG — 1.5
SALT/PEPPER — 1
VANILLA — 0.5
OFF
(tsp)

ICE

3
2
1
OFF
(scoops)

GLASS

CHAMPANGE
MARTINI
HIGHBALL
MUG
SHOT
CORDIAL
SHERRY
OLD FASHIONED

GARNISH

LEMON TW.
LEMON WD.
LIME
CHERRY
OLIVE
ONION

PREPARATION
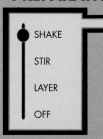

SHAKE
STIR
LAYER
OFF

hard
medium
soft
OFF

SALT RIM
SUGAR RIM
WHIPPED CREAM
OFF

Preset Drinks

LONG ISLAND ICE TEA

BLOODY MARY

SANGRIA

MIX IT

BIBLIOGRAPHY

Bénitah, Thierry. *The Little Book of Whisky*. Paris: Flammarion, 2001.

Dikty, Alan S., editor. *Beverage Tasting Institute's Buying Guide to Spirits*. New York: Sterling Publishing, 1999.

Calabrese, Salvatore. *Classic Cocktails*. New York: Sterling Publishing, 1997.

Collins, Philip. *The Art of the Cocktail*. San Francisco: Chronicle Books, 1992.

Conrad III, Barnaby. *The Martini*. San Francisco: Chronicle Books, 1995.

Faith, Nicholas. *Classic Brandy*. London: Prion Books Ltd., 2000.

Gabányi, Stefan. *Whisk(e)y*. New York: Abbeville Press, 1997.

Greenberg, Emanuel and Madeline. *The Pocket Guide to Spirits & Liqueurs*. New York: Perigee Books, 1983.

MacNeil, Karen. *The Wine Bible*. New York: Workman Publishing, 2001.

Pacult, F. Paul. *Kindred Spirits*. New York: Hyperion, 1997.

Pessey, Christian. *The Little Book of Cognac*. Paris: Flammarion, 2002.

Regan, Gary. *The Bartender's Bible*. New York: Harper Collins Publishers, 1991.

Schumann, Charles. *American Bar*. New York: Abbeville Press, 1995.

Schumann, Charles. *Tropical Bar Book*. New York: Stewart, Tabori & Chang, 1989.

Spalding, Jill. *Blithe Spirits*. Washington, D.C.: Rosenbaum/Acropolis Books, 1988.

Thompson, Jennifer Trainer. *Caribbean Cocktails*. Berkeley: Ten Speed Press, 2003.

Waggoner, Susan, and Robert Markel. *Vintage Cocktails*. New York: Stewart, Tabori & Chang, 1999.

William-Sonoma, Ray Foley, editor. *The Bar Guide*. Time-Life Books, 1999

INDEX

gin in, 25–26
tequila in, 58, 62
vodka in, 33–35
whiskey in, 36, 49, 50–53
See also Prohibitionism

V
Van Gogh, Vincent, 111
vanilla schnapps, 110
Velvet Hammer, 109
vermouth, 94, 117–18
  in Americano, 157
  in Arnaud, 159
  in Havana Club, 168
  in Manhattans, 155
  in Martinis, 148, 152–53
  in Parisian, 174
  in Rolls Royce, 175
Versinthe (pastis), 112
Villas, James, 154
Vincelli, Bernardo, 103
Virgin Islands rum, 74
vodka
  basic facts, 20
  etymology of, 30–33
  flavored, 20, 35
  gin compared to, 20, 22
  historical overview of, 30–35
  invention of, 30
  legal definition of, 30
  popularity of, 30
  as potato-based, 20, 33
  premium brands, 20, 35
vodka cocktails
  Absolut Redhead, 157
  Black Russian, 179
  Bloody Mary, 162
  Bull Shot, 161
  Cape Codder, 161
  Coffee Cooler, 161
  Cosmopolitan, 164
  Count Stroganoff, 164
  Dirty Girl Scout, 164
  Dubonnet Fizz, 165
  Gimlet, 165
  Godmother, 167
  Greyhound, 167
  Harvey Wallbanger, 167
  Ice Pick, 168

  Kurant Cassis, 171
  Lemon Drop, 171
  Moscow Mule, 173
  Mudslide, 173
  Red Caipiroshka, 175
  Screwdriver, 176
  Sea Breeze, 176
  Vodka Collins, 35
  White Russian, 179
Volstead Act (1920), 49, 124–25

W
whipped cream, 129
whiskey cocktails
  Hot Toddy, 168
  Irish Coffee, 168
  Manhattan, 155
  Mint Julep, 172
  Old-Fashioned, 173
  Whiskey Sour, 179
Whiskey Sour, 179
whiskey/whisky
  American, 50–53
  basic facts, 36
  blended, 52
  body of, 45
  Canadian, 55
  determining quality of, 39
  distilling process, 38–39
  historical overview of, 38
  Irish, 49
  Scotch, 40–46
  smell of, 54
  sour mash, 52–53
  spelling discrepancy, 44
  straight, 53
White Burner, 179
White Lady, 179
White Russian, 108, 179
William III (king of England), 25
Willis, Bruce, 5
wormwood, 112, 117

Y
Youngman, Henny, 24

Z
zesters, 138
Zombie, 74, 179

Please visit our website, **www.whoisitanyway.com**, for lists of our favorite spirits, updates, recipes, stories, bar lore, and more.